WHAT TO DO WHEN SOMEONE DIES

What to do when someone dies

a Consumer Publication

Consumers' Association
publishers of **Which?**
14 Buckingham Street
London WC2N 6DS

a Consumer Publication

edited by   Edith Rudinger

published by   Consumers' Association
publishers of **Which?**

Consumer Publications are
available from Consumers'
Association and from
booksellers. Details of
other Consumer Publications
are given at the end of
this book.

© Consumers' Association 1967
revised (9th) edition November 1978
revised reprint December 1980
                October 1982
                November 1983

ISBN 0 85202 156 9
      0 340 23139 4
        Printed in Great Britain

        by Page Bros
        (Norwich) Ltd.

CONTENTS

The book deals with the formalities and procedure in England and Wales; the important differences which apply in Scotland are given on pages 29–34 and on pages 93–94.

This book aims to help those who have never had to deal with the arrangements that must be made after a death—getting a doctor's certificate and registering the death, deciding whether to bury or cremate, choosing an undertaker and a coffin, putting notices in the papers, selecting the form of service, claiming national insurance benefits. It explains the function of people with whom they will come in contact, often for the first time. They will get help and guidance from the doctor, the registrar, the undertaker, the clergyman, the cemetery or crematorium officials, the Department of Health and Social Security and, in some circumstances, the police and the coroner. However, it is the executor or nearest relative who has to make the decisions, often at a time of personal distress. *What to do when someone dies* describes what needs to be done, when, and how to set about it.

No attempt is made to deal with the personal or social aspects of death, such as the psychology of grief and shock, the rituals and conventions of mourning, or attitudes to death.

You may discover someone apparently dead, and it can be difficult to tell whether he really is dead or not. For instance, someone rescued from water may appear not to breathe, yet might be revived by artificial respiration.

The body temperature drops at the rate of one to two degrees centigrade an hour for the first few hours after death, so someone who has been dead for an hour or so is appreciably colder than normal. The extremities—feet and hands—get cold first. But very low body temperature alone is not a sure sign of death because comatose or unconscious people can also seem abnormally cold.

Telling the doctor
If there is any doubt whether someone is dead, treat him as being still alive. The first thing to do is to call the doctor. If you do not know how or where to get hold of a doctor, dial '999' for the emergency ambulance service.

Even if it seems certain that the person really is dead, you should let his doctor know soon. But if the doctor had been in attendance and the death was not unexpected, there may be no need to telephone him in the middle of the night instead of waiting until the next morning. Ask whether the doctor is going to come. If the death was peaceful and expected, the doctor may not feel it necessary to see the body, or may not come straightaway. Some doctors make it a practice to see the body of every patient who has died.

You should tell the doctor if the body is to be cremated because, if so, the doctor will have to examine the body and arrange for another doctor to do so, too. If the body is not to be cremated, you can straightaway ask an undertaker to come to take the body away or to lay it out; he may charge for this service.

Laying out the body

Rigor mortis, a stiffening of the muscles, usually begins within about 6 hours after death, and gradually extends over the whole body in about 18 hours, after which it begins to wear off. Rigor mortis is less pronounced in the body of an old person. When someone has been dead for about half an hour or more, parts of the skin will have started to discolour. This discoloration, which is called post mortem staining, is caused by the blood sinking under the action of gravity.

Laying out, usually done by a nurse or by one of the undertaker's staff, should be done as soon as possible. The body is washed, the natural orifices stopped up with cotton wool and a napkin, and clean clothes put on. The eyelids are closed and the jaw supported, the hair is tidied and the arms and feet put straight. A man may need to be shaved. When the laying out is done at home, the person laying out usually brings most of the necessary equipment, but may ask to be given a sheet and some towels, a pillow, warm water, soap and disinfectant, and perhaps a nightdress or pyjamas or a shirt to put on the body.

If someone has died quietly and expectedly at home and in bed, it is all right to tidy the room and rearrange or lay out the body. But if you discover a dead body in any other circumstances, do as little as possible to it until the doctor comes. Do not move it unless it is likely to be damaged or cause damage where it is.

Calling the police

If you think that death appears to have been caused by an accident or violence, or to have occurred in other suspicious circumstances, you should at once inform the police. Do not touch or move anything in the room, nor allow anyone else to do so, until the police say that you may. The police will almost certainly want to take statements from anyone who was with the deceased when he died, or who discovered the body, but no one is obliged to give a statement to the police. If there is an inquest later, anyone who has made a statement may be called as a witness, as may any person whom the coroner believes may be able to give information about the death.

If a body cannot be immediately identified, the police circulate a description in police journals, and occasionally to the general press, too. Anyone who might be able to identify the body usually has to go to the mortuary with the police to do so.

If the police are called and no relative or other person responsible is immediately available, the police take possession of any cash or valuables. As a general rule, this property is given up to whoever can later prove his right to it. The police also take away any article which may have a bearing on the cause of death—a letter or bottle of pills, for example—in case this is needed by the coroner.

Medical certificate of cause of death

The law requires that every death in this country shall be registered. For this, medical evidence of the cause of death must be given. The person who has authority to do so is either the coroner or the doctor who was looking after the deceased during the final illness. More usually, it is the doctor who issues a medical certificate of cause of death. On the medical certificate, the doctor states to the best of his knowledge and belief the cause or causes of death, the last date on which he had seen the deceased alive, and whether or not a doctor has seen the body. The doctor is not allowed to charge for this certificate.

The doctor either gives the certificate to one of the deceased's relatives to take to the registrar of the area in which the death took place or he sends it to the registrar direct. On the back of the certificate the doctor indicates if he has reported the case to the coroner.

When a death has been reported to the coroner, the registrar cannot register the death until the coroner authorises him to do so.

The coroner

The office of the coroner was instituted in England in norman times. He was the king's officer appointed for a shire or a borough for the purpose of keeping an eye on the sheriff, keeping a record of all sudden deaths (that is, deaths which were 'against the course of nature') and of any occurrence by which monies or property might be forfeit and revert to the crown.

Nowadays the coroner is a qualified doctor or lawyer, sometimes both. He is appointed by the metropolitan or county council but is responsible to no one except the crown. Some of his duties are now largely archaic, such as instituting inquiries regarding the finding of any gold or silver whose ownership is unknown in order to discover whether it is treasure trove and therefore belongs to the crown. His main function is to investigate any death which has been reported to him.

A death has to be reported to the coroner if the doctor had not attended the deceased at all during his last illness. Even if the doctor had been treating him, if he had not seen him within the last 14 days, the death will have to be reported to the coroner unless the doctor comes to see the body. (In Northern Ireland, the period within which the doctor should have last seen the patient is 28 days.)

Any death that was sudden must be reported to the coroner; also a death caused either directly or indirectly by any kind of accident, if the circumstances of the death are in any way suspicious (such as violence or neglect), and if the medical cause is unknown.

The coroner must be notified of any death which takes place during an operation, and if death follows an operation required after an injury. Suicides, and deaths which may have been caused by an abortion, by drugs, alcoholism or cirrhosis of the liver, or by poisoning (including food poisoning) must be reported. So must a death attributable to what is classified as an industrial disease, and in some cases one caused or accelerated by an injury received during military service.

Generally, it is the doctor who reports a death to the coroner, or the police. The registrar of births and deaths will do so if the cause or circumstances of the death warrant it. But anyone who is uneasy about the apparent cause of a death has the right to inform the coroner for the district. By telephoning a police station, you can find out who is the coroner for the relevant district and how to get in touch with him. This is usually through the coroner's officer, who is almost always a police officer. There may be some circumstances which you feel are contributory to the death but may not be known to the doctor—such as an old war wound or injury—which can be established by a post mortem examination.

Reporting a death to the coroner does not inevitably mean a post mortem or an inquest, although the majority of deaths reported to a coroner do lead to a post mortem; about one-fifth lead to an inquest. This varies from district to district because it is up to each individual coroner to decide what action shall be taken.

If, after considering the circumstances of a death, the coroner decides that there is no need for further investigation, he sends a formal notice of his decision to the registrar of the district. If the registrar knows who the next of kin are he gets in touch with them and tells them that he is now in a position to register the death. If the death had been reported to the coroner direct, the registrar will not know who the next of kin are, so he has to wait until someone comes to him.

Post mortem
A post mortem examination is usually ordered to establish with certainty the medical cause of death. It may be important to be able to state the medical cause of death

accurately if there are any legal proceedings arising from the death.

If the coroner decides that a post mortem is required, it will be carried out even if it is against the wishes of the relatives or the religion of the deceased. The coroner's officer becomes responsible for the body, and has it removed to the mortuary if it is not already there.

If the post mortem reveals that the death was due to a natural cause and no other circumstances warrant further investigation, the coroner notifies the registrar. The coroner has no duty to inform the next of kin of the result of the post mortem. In some districts, the coroner's officer or another policeman calls on the family to tell them; otherwise, the next of kin have to enquire at the registrar's office every few days to find out whether the coroner's notification has arrived, or get the undertaker to find out.

After the post mortem, the body becomes again the responsibility of the family, unless there is to be an inquest.

Inquest

The coroner can choose to hold an inquest on any death reported to him. But if he has reasonable grounds for suspecting that the death was violent or unnatural, he is legally obliged to hold an inquest. He is also obliged to hold one when a person has died in circumstances where the law requires an inquest to be held—for example, in prison or following a road accident.

An inquest is held to establish who the deceased was,

how, when and where he died, and any other particulars required for the registration of the death.

Inquests are formal proceedings to which the public are generally admitted. To find out when and where an inquest is being held, ask at the police station nearest the place of death or telephone the local coroner's office.

A coroner's court is a court of law, even though no one is accused. Witnesses are on oath. The coroner can admit any evidence, including, if he sees fit, hearsay evidence which in other courts of law might be inadmissible. The coroner may call any person who can give information about the death: for instance, someone who made a statement to the police about it. A policeman will have gone round beforehand to tell witnesses the date, place and time of the inquest. If anyone who has been requested to come as a witness says that he will not attend the inquest, he will be officially instructed by the coroner to do so and a coroner's summons can be served to make sure the witness will come. Witnesses can claim from the court compensation for expenses and loss of time.

There is a minimum amount of pomp and ceremony at an inquest. The coroner calls witnesses in turn from the main part of the court to come up to the witness box. Each witness swears or affirms that he 'will speak the truth, the whole truth and nothing but the truth'. The taking of the oath is the only formal element in the proceedings.

First the coroner questions the witness, then, with his permission, the witness can be examined by anyone present who has a legal interest in the case (or by that person's legal representative). You have such an interest, for instance, if the person who was killed was a close relative, but not if you are the secretary of the Society for the Abolition of Road Traffic and want to speak in the case of a motor accident. When all the witnesses have been heard, the coroner sums up. If you know you will want to give evidence or examine a witness, tell the coroner's officer beforehand, so that the coroner can call you at the right moment. You should speak before the coroner has summed up.

There should be no expense to the family arising out of the inquest, unless the services of a solicitor are needed. Many people think it wise for the family to be represented by a solicitor in a case of death resulting from an accident or occupational disease, because there may be compensation claims to be made later and a solicitor would be better able to make use of the evidence presented at an inquest.

Some inquests must be held with a jury. This applies to a death due to a rail or air accident or resulting from an industrial accident or disease. An inquiry into the death of a person in custody must be held with a jury, even in cases where the death is due to natural causes. In all other cases, it is up to the coroner to decide whether to hold the inquest with or without a jury.

The jury for an inquest consists of not less than seven and not more than eleven men or women eligible for jury service. The jurors are on oath. Although the coroner must view the body, the jurors need not unless the coroner directs them to.

At the end of his summing up, the coroner directs the

jury as to the law and the possible verdicts they may
bring in. A majority verdict is acceptable, provided that
not more than two of the jurors dissent. Each member
tells the foreman what he thinks and the foreman tells
the coroner their joint verdict. The jury do not usually
leave the court to discuss their decision but may do so.
If there is no jury, the coroner gives his verdict at the
end of his summing up of the case.

If criminal proceedings have been started against some
person charged with causing death by reckless driving,
with murder, manslaughter or infanticide of the deceased
or with aiding, abetting or procuring his suicide, the
coroner is required by law to adjourn the inquest pending
the conclusion of those proceedings. Within five days of
adjourning the inquest, the coroner must send to the
registrar of births and deaths a certificate giving the
particulars required for the death to be registered.

In other cases, where the coroner adjourns the inquest
at his own discretion—for instance, to await the result
of an inquiry into an air crash or other disaster—the
coroner can provide a letter stating that the inquest has
been postponed, to allow any insurance or other payments to be claimed and the estate to be administered.

When the coroner adjourns an inquest, whether for
criminal proceedings to take place or for further investigations to be made, he is able to give his authority for
the body to be buried or cremated: the coroner gives or
sends to the next of kin or other responsible person, a
certificate for cremation or an order for burial, whichever
is required.

In all cases other than those involving a serious crime,

registration of the death takes place after the inquest when the coroner sends a certificate after inquest to the registrar of births and deaths of the district in which the death took place or in which the body was found. This certificate provides the registrar with the information he requires to register the death.

Registering

If there has been an inquest, the details in the coroner's certificate after inquest are all the registrar needs. In all other cases, someone has to give him the information necessary for registering the death, and has to sign the register.

In this country, deaths should be registered within five days of death. Registration can be delayed for a further nine days provided the registrar receives, in writing, confirmation that a medical certificate of cause of death has been signed by the doctor.

Under english law, all deaths must be registered in the registration sub-district in which they took place or in which the body was found. A list of names, addresses and telephone numbers of local registrars is usually displayed in doctors' surgeries, in post offices, and in public libraries and other public buildings, together with their office hours and a description of the sub-district they cover.

Usually, whoever is giving the information goes in person to the registrar's office. Very few registration districts have an appointment system; normally you just go along during the registrar's office hours and wait until he is free to see you.

The law defines who qualifies to give the required information to the registrar. Attached to the doctor's medical certificate of cause of death is a 'notice to informant', with a list of people who can act as informant. If the death occurred in a house or inside any other building, the informant can be a relative who was present at the death or during the last illness, or a relative who lives, or happens to be, in the sub-district of the registrar for the deceased. If there is no eligible relative, the informant may be any other person who was present at the death; the head of the household (in a public institution, the senior resident officer); anyone else living in the house who knew about the death; or the person responsible for making the funeral arrangements.

If the person had been found dead out of doors, the informant could be a relative who has enough information about the deceased to complete the details for the registrar; anyone who happened to be there when the person died or who found the body; or whoever is in charge of the body (this will be the police if the body cannot be identified) or responsible for making the funeral arrangements.

The responsibility of being an informant must not be delegated to anyone not qualified to act. The doctor should give the 'notice to informant' to the person who is going to be the informant, who should take it to the registrar. If he does not have the medical evidence of the cause of death (because the doctor is posting the medical certificate direct to the registrar), the informant should allow time for the evidence to reach the registrar before he goes to register the death. If the registrar finds that the information the doctor has been able to give on the medical certificate of cause of death is inadequate, he will have to report the death to the coroner. He will also do so if he sees that the death was due to some cause which makes it reportable.

The procedure for registering a death is a simple question-and-answer interview between the registrar and the informant. The registrar will, first of all, make sure that the death took place in his sub-district; he cannot register a death which occurred in any place outside his jurisdiction. He will ask in what capacity whoever is registering the death qualifies to be the informant—relative, present at the death, or other reason.

He then fills in a draft form for the register of deaths with details of the informant, the date of death and exactly where it occurred, the name and surname of the dead person. It is as well to give all the names by which the deceased had ever been known, so that there can be no doubt who the particulars refer to. In order to avoid difficulties over identity in connection with probate, insurance policies, pensions and bank accounts, the names should be the same as those on birth and marriage certificates, and on any other relevant documents. The maiden surname of a married woman is required. The sex of the dead person, date and place of birth, and address are entered. For someone who died away from home, the home address should be given.

Next, the registrar will ask what was the last full-time occupation of the deceased, and whether he or she was retired at the time of death. The description of the occupation should be precise: 'miner' could be anyone from a geologist prospecting for diamond-bearing rock strata in the african veldt to a colliery pithead baths attendant.

A woman who was married or widowed at the time of her death, in addition to her own occupation or profession, would be described as 'wife of' or 'widow of', followed by the name and occupation of her husband. A woman who had never been married or a woman whose marriage had been dissolved would have her occupation recorded, with no reference to her marital status.

Children under the age of sixteen are described as 'son of' or 'daughter of', followed by the names and occupations of the parents. If the child was illegitimate and paternity had not been established, the name of the mother only is entered.

The registrar copies the medical cause of death from the doctor's certificate or the coroner's notification, and adds the name and qualification of the doctor or coroner.

On the draft form, but not in the register itself, the registrar enters the deceased's national health service number or his date of birth. If the deceased was over sixteen years old, additional information is requested: marital status at the time of death (single, married, widowed or divorced) and the age of any widow or widower left. This information is not entered in the register in England and Wales, and is used only for the preparation of population statistics by the registrar general.

The informant should check the draft of the proposed entry in the register to make sure that there is nothing wrong or misleading in it. When the particulars are agreed, the registrar makes the entry in the register itself and asks the informant to check and sign it. The informant should sign his usual signature, even if this is not his whole name. The registrar has to use special ink for the register, so sign with the pen he offers.

After adding the date of the registration, the registrar himself signs the entry in the final space. Any errors can be corrected without formality before the entry has been signed, but once it is signed by the registrar, the entry cannot be corrected without the authority of the registrar general, who may require documentary evidence to justify the correction.

FOR REGISTRATION—THE DOCUMENTS

notice to informant	from doctor	gives details of who must register death and what particulars will be required	via relative to registrar
medical certificate of cause of death	from doctor	states cause of death	to registrar (direct or via relative)
if coroner involved: coroner's notification	from coroner	confirms or gives details of cause of death	direct to registrar
or coroner's certificate after inquest	from coroner	gives all the particulars required for death to be registered	direct to registrar

The registrar can now let you have copies of the entry in the register (the death certificates) which you may need for probate and other purposes.

Make a note of the number of the entry in the register and the date, and of the registration district, because you may need more copies of the entry later.

At the time of registering the death, the registrar will ask for the deceased's medical card. If the informant has not brought it, the registrar will give him a pre-paid addressed envelope to send it later. This is to enable the national health service register to be kept up to date.

Death certificates

A document which confirms the registration of the death is needed in order to claim the various national insurance benefits after someone has died. The registrar issues this when registering the death. This certificate of registration is free and is of use only for claiming national insurance benefits. The application form for claiming (form BD8) is printed on the back of the certificate. If registration of the death has had to be delayed for any reason, the registrar amends the certificate of registration to a certificate of notification of death, provided he has received the necessary evidence of death from the doctor or coroner. If the delay is due to an inquest being held, and the next of kin need to claim any payments or benefits straightaway, they can ask the coroner for a written statement to use in place of a death certificate.

The other certificates you will need when making arrangements about the deceased's affairs are all certified copies of the entry of death in the register—death certificates. A 'standard' death certificate is the one for sending with an application for a grant of probate or letters of administration. It costs £1·80 in England and Wales.

There is a specific certificate costing £1·50 for claiming from a registered friendly society (or the standard £1·80 death certificate can be used). To obtain this £1·50 certificate, you must tell the registrar the name of the friendly society concerned. You may not know from the name of the society or company whether it is an industrial assurance company or a friendly society, but if you take the policies or a list of the full titles with you to the registrar, he should be able to tell you.

Neither the standard certificate nor the friendly society certificate will be accepted for claims in connection with insurance taken out on the life of a parent or grandparent by a child, adopted child, stepchild or grandchild. A special certificate, also costing £1·50, must be obtained for this. On the application form for this certificate, the applicant certifies that he had taken out an insurance on the life of the deceased parent or grandparent and states his relationship. Unlike other death certificates, it is solely for the use of the applicant whose name and address is given. Only one of these special death certificates is issued to any one person. If more than one insurance company is involved, the certificate should be reclaimed after each company has endorsed it. If the original certificate is lost or destroyed, a duplicate can only be obtained if the applicant makes a statutory declaration in front of a JP, magistrate, commissioner for oaths or a practising solicitor.

Yet another form of death certificate, also costing £1·50, is issued for 'certain other statutory purposes' for claiming under various national insurance and social security acts. This death certificate can be used instead of the free certificate of registration of the death (incorporating form BD8) for claiming national insurance benefits, if the BD8 certificate has been lost. In cases where probate is not required, this is the certificate needed for encashing national savings certificates, premium savings bonds, national savings bank deposits at the post office or trustee savings bank deposits.

DEATH CERTIFICATES (England and Wales)

certificate of registration/ notification of death (incorporating form BD8)	free	for claiming death grant and widow's benefit from the Department of Health and Social Security
standard death certificate	£1·80	for obtaining probate; for private claims such as life insurance and pension schemes; also for friendly societies
special death certificate	£1·50	for claiming insurance taken out on the life of a parent or grandparent
certificate for purposes of Friendly Societies Acts	£1·50	for claiming from a registered friendly society
certificate for certain statutory purposes	£1·50	for claiming under the national insurance and social security acts, or if the certificate of registration of death has been lost; when probate is not required, for claiming on trustee savings banks, national savings banks, national savings certificates and premium savings bonds.

If you want the registrar to advise you about the number and type of certificates you may need, take with you a list of the various purposes for which you think some evidence of the death may be required. You can get further copies of certificates if any come to be needed later on.

If you need a standard death certificate later on, the certificate will cost you £4·60. If the death was fairly recent, you apply to the registrar who registered it. If the death was registered more than about a year previously, standard death certificates can be obtained from the General Register Office, St Catherines House, 10 Kingsway, London WC2B 6JP. The charge is £4·60 if you go in person to St Catherines House; £9·60 if you apply by post.

If you need to apply for certificates from the registrar of another district, your local registrar can tell you the names and addresses of all other registrars. He can give you the application forms needed for the various certificates and help you to complete them. With any postal application for a certificate, you must send the necessary cheque or postal order and a stamped addressed envelope. When you get certificates from your local registrar in person, you are expected to pay there and then.

In Northern Ireland, the General Register Office address is Oxford House, 49–55 Chichester Street, Belfast BT1 4HL, and the charge for a standard death certificate is £3·50. The special death certificates for insurance purposes cost £1.

Death in hospital
When death has taken place in a hospital or similar institution, what happens up to the time of registering is slightly different from the arrangements that have to be made if a person has died at home.

The next of kin are informed by the ward sister. If death was unexpected or the result of an accident, it may be the police who find and tell the next of kin. A member of the family is asked to come to the hospital and, if the dead person was not already a patient in the hospital, may have to identify the body, usually not in the mortuary but by being shown the body in another room.

Hospitals differ from each other in procedure but it is usually the administrative rather than the medical staff who make the arrangements with the relatives; in some hospitals it is one of the head porter's duties, in others the relatives may have to deal with several people. Whoever goes to the hospital may be asked to take away the deceased's possessions, so it is as well to take along a suitcase. A shroud will be provided under the national health service, if required.

Hospitals often want to carry out a post mortem examination to find out more about the cause of death. The hospital cannot carry out such a post mortem without the permission of the deceased's next of kin. The person who goes to the hospital following a death should therefore be prepared to say whether the next of kin will allow the hospital to carry out a post mortem, and, if so, to sign a consent form. Relatives are told the result of the post mortem, if they want to know.

The medical certificate of cause of death is usually

completed by the hospital doctor. However, if the person had died before a hospital doctor had a chance to diagnose the case, the dead person's own doctor is asked to issue the medical certificate. If he cannot, the hospital will report the death to the coroner. A hospital will also report to the coroner a death that took place when the patient was undergoing an operation, or was under the effects of anaesthesia or in any other circumstances which have to be reported. The responsibility for the body is then transferred from the hospital to the coroner, and the coroner's office not the hospital is where the relatives should then seek information.

If the certificate of cause of death can be issued at the hospital and the death is not being reported to the coroner, the family has to arrange for the body to be taken away from the hospital mortuary. If the body is to be cremated, the necessary medical forms will be completed at the hospital; the doctors can charge for this.

The procedure for registering the death is the same as for an ordinary death at home, but the registration must be done at the office of the registrar in whose district the hospital is.

Stillbirths

The process of registering a stillbirth is a mixture of registering a birth and registering a death and has to be done within 42 days. People qualified to register a stillbirth are (as for live births): the mother; the father if the child would have been legitimate had it been born alive; the occupier of the house or other premises in which the stillbirth occurred; a person who was present at the stillbirth or who found the stillborn child.

A stillborn child is a child born after the 28th week of pregnancy which did not at any time breathe or show any other signs of life. Foetal death before the 28th week does not fall within the legal definition of a stillbirth and is usually considered a miscarriage.

If a doctor was in attendance at a stillbirth or examined the body of the stillborn child, he gives a certificate of stillbirth, stating the cause of death and the duration of the pregnancy. A certified midwife can issue the certificate if no doctor was there. If no doctor or midwife was in attendance at, or after, the birth, one of the parents, or someone who was in the house at the time, can make a declaration on a form (form 35, available from the registrar of births and deaths), saying that to the best of his or her knowledge and belief the child was stillborn. If there is any doubt whether the child was born alive or not, the case must be reported to the coroner of the district, who may then order a post mortem or an inquest and will issue a certificate of the cause of death when he has completed his inquiries.

When registering a stillbirth, the registrar has to have the doctor's or midwife's certificate, or a declaration of the stillbirth. Whoever goes to register has to tell the registrar the name, surname and maiden name of the mother, her place of birth and her usual residence at the time of the child's birth, and if she had never been married, also her occupation. If the child would have been legitimate, the name, surname and occupation of the father and his place of birth are required. If the father and mother are married to each other, the registrar asks the month and year of the marriage, and the number of the mother's previous children, both born alive and stillborn, by her present and any former husband; this information is needed for statistical purposes only in order to forecast population trends and is not entered in the register.

Disposal certificate

Once a death has been registered, the registrar can issue a certificate, referred to generally as the disposal certificate, authorising either burial or application for cremation. A body cannot be buried or cremated without this certificate or its equivalent, namely the coroner's order for burial or certificate for cremation. It is unwise to make more than provisional arrangements for the funeral until you have a certificate for disposal.

You will get authority to dispose of the body from the registrar or from the coroner but not from both. If the death has been reported to the coroner, only he can give a certificate authorising cremation; if the body is to be buried, the registrar can issue the disposal certificate. However, if there has been an inquest, it is the coroner who issues either an order for burial or a certificate for cremation.

No fee is charged for a disposal certificate. If you lose it, you or the burial or crematorium officials have to apply to the registrar or the coroner who issued the original certificate for a duplicate. There is no charge for this duplicate.

Once you have obtained a certificate for disposal from the registrar or the coroner, give it to the undertaker who will take it to the church, cemetery or crematorium officials. Without it, they will not bury or cremate a body. It is the responsibility of the church, cemetery or crematorium to complete part C of the disposal certificate and to return it to the registrar. If the registrar does not receive it within 14 days of the certificate having been issued, he will get in touch with the person to whom the disposal certificate had been given to find out what is happening. Unless a satisfactory reply is received, the registrar reports the facts to the local environmental health officer, who will investigate the case. He may then, if circumstances warrant, remove the body for disposal.

The registrar can issue a disposal certificate before registering a death but only when he has already received the requisite information (including medical evidence) and is just waiting for the informant to come and register the death. This may arise, for instance, when the only suitable informant is ill in hospital but the funeral has to take place. A disposal certificate issued by the registrar before registration authorises burial only; crematorium authorities are not allowed to accept such a certificate.

Medical certificate of cause of death

The medical certificate of cause of death given by doctors in Scotland is similar to that in England. The obligation to give the certificate rests on the doctor who attended the deceased during his last illness but, if there was no doctor in attendance, the certificate may be issued by any doctor who is able to do so. The doctor hands the certificate to a relative to take to the local registrar or sends it direct to the registrar. In the majority of cases, the certificate is issued to a relative. The people who can act as informant include relatives of the deceased, his legal representative or, failing any of these, any other person who has knowledge of the particulars to be registered.

If a medical certificate of cause of death cannot be given, the registrar can, nevertheless, register the death but must report the facts of the case to the procurator fiscal.

The procurator fiscal

There are no coroners in Scotland and the duties which in England would be carried out by a coroner are in Scotland carried out by a procurator fiscal. The procurator fiscal is a full-time law officer, who comes under the Lord Advocate.

The procurator fiscal has many functions, including responsibility for investigating all unexpected and violent deaths and also any death which occurred under suspicious circumstances. If he is satisfied with the doctor's medical certificate and any evidence he receives from the police, he need take no further action. If, however, the procurator fiscal considers a further medical report is necessary, he requests a medical practitioner (frequently a police surgeon) to report to him 'on soul and conscience' what he considers was the cause of death. In the majority of cases, a post mortem is not carried out and the doctor certifies the cause of death after an external examination. The mere fact that the cause of death is in a medical sense unexplained is not a ground for ordering a dissection at the public expense, provided the intrinsic circumstances sufficiently explain the cause of death in a popular sense and do not raise a suspicion of criminality or negligence. In cases where the procurator fiscal decides a post mortem is necessary, permission to carry it out is given by the sheriff. One doctor is usually sufficient but if, while conducting the dissection, the doctor finds unexpected difficulties, the procurator fiscal may decide to bring in a second doctor in order to be able to certify the cause of death. In all cases where there is a possibility of criminal proceedings being taken against someone and it is necessary to prove the fact and cause of death, a post mortem should be carried out by two medical practitioners.

Death while in legal custody or as the result of an accident during work must be the subject of a public inquiry, which takes the place of an inquest in England. If a person has died of natural causes while engaged in industrial employment or occupation, there may, but will not necessarily, be a public inquiry.

Unlike in England where a coroner himself decides what he shall or shall not do, in Scotland the procurator fiscal reports certain cases to the crown office and it is the Lord Advocate who makes the final decision about whether to apply to a sheriff for an inquiry to be held. In all other cases, investigations made into sudden deaths are carried out by the procurator fiscal confidentially.

Before reporting a case to the crown office, unless there is a likelihood of criminal proceedings being taken, the procurator fiscal interviews witnesses and the relatives in private (this is called a precognition).

Cases which are reported to the crown office because they may result in a public inquiry are those where there is an issue of public interest at stake—for instance, to prevent a recurrence of similar circumstances—and deaths following a road accident or otherwise directly or indirectly connected with the action of a third party.

A public inquiry in Scotland is heard before the sheriff in the local sheriff court. The procurator fiscal examines the witnesses but it is the sheriff who determines the circumstances of the death.

When he has completed his investigations, the procurator fiscal notifies the result of his findings to the registrar general. If the death has already been registered, the registrar general lets the local registrar know if any changes need to made to the entry. If the death has not already been registered, the registrar general instructs the registrar of the district in which the death occurred to register the death.

Registering
In Scotland, the law requires that every death must be registered within 8 days from the date of death.

The person qualified to act as informant for registering a death is any relative of the deceased, any person present at the death, the deceased's executor or other legal representative, the occupier of the premises where the death took place, or any person having knowledge of the particulars to be registered.

While in England a death must be registered in the registration office for the district in which the death occurred, in Scotland the death may be registered either in the office for the district in which the death occurred or in the office for the district in which the deceased had normally resided before his death, provided this was also in Scotland. The death of a visitor to Scotland must be registered where the death took place.

As in England, the procedure for registering a death is a simple question-and-answer interview between registrar and informant. The registrar will demand the production of a medical certificate of cause of death or, failing that, the name and address of a doctor who can be asked to give the certificate. The information required by a scottish registrar to register a death is much the same as in England and Wales, except that he also needs to know the time of death; if the deceased had ever been married, the name, surname and occupation of each spouse; the name and occupation of the deceased's father and the name and maiden surname of the mother, and whether the parents are alive or dead.

When the form of particulars has been completed, the registrar asks the informant to read it over carefully to ensure that all the particulars are correct, and to sign it. The registrar then makes the entry in the register and asks the informant to check it carefully and sign the entry before he adds the date and his own signature.

Stillbirths

A stillbirth in Scotland must be registered within 21 days. As in England, if no doctor or midwife can issue a certificate of stillbirth, an informant must make a declaration on a special form. In Scotland, this is form 7, obtainable from the registrar. All such cases, and any case where there is doubt as to whether the child was alive or not, are reported to the procurator fiscal who notifies the registrar general of the results of his investigations.

If the body is to be cremated, a certificate of stillbirth must be given by the doctor who was in attendance at the confinement (or who conducted a post mortem). The stillbirth must have been registered before cremation can take place.

A stillbirth can be registered either in the district in which it took place or in the district in Scotland in which the mother of the stillborn child was ordinarily resident at the time of the stillbirth.

The informant must produce to the registrar a doctor's or midwife's certificate, or the completed form 7, and is required to give the same information as in England and, in addition, the time of the stillbirth and, where applicable, the place of the parents' marriage.

Certificate of registration

There is no direct equivalent in Scotland of a disposal certificate. After registration, the registrar issues to the informant a certificate of registration of death, which should be given to the undertaker to give to the keeper of the burial ground or to the crematorium authorities. There is no charge for this certificate.

Death certificates

As in England, the registrar issues, free of charge, a certificate of registration of death which can be used for national insurance purposes only. All other death certificates must be paid for.

The full copy of an entry in the death register (the standard death certificate) costs £1.80 if applied for within seven days of the date of registration. If applied for at a later date, the charge is £4.60. Each further copy of the same entry ordered at the same time costs £1.80.

The other death certificates cost the same as in England. There are a number of different certificates for various special purposes similar to those in England.

In order to get the death certificate for claiming from a trustee savings bank, you must provide the registrar with a statement, signed by an officer of the bank, that the certificate is required for savings bank purposes.

Death certificates are always obtainable from the registrar of the district where the death was registered; they are also obtainable from the General Register Office for Scotland, New Register House, Edinburgh EH1 3YT, at any time after about a year to 18 months from the date of registration. The same fees are charged whether the application is made personally or by post.

In this country, the dead are either buried or cremated.

If the deceased has left no specific instructions, the decision what to do with the dead body is normally made by the executor or the next of kin. If there is neither, the person entrusted by the hospital or local authority to deal with the funeral arrangements has to decide about the disposal of the body. If you put any directions about the disposal of your body in your will, also tell your executors or nearest kin, in case the will is not read until after the funeral. Although it is usual to carry out any wishes the deceased had expressed about the disposal of his body, there is no legal obligation to do so.

Bequest of eyes
Corneal grafting is a technique of modern eye surgery which helps to cure blindness or defective sight. People wishing to bequeath their eyes for this purpose can write to the secretary of their nearest eye hospital, or to the Royal National Institute for the Blind (RNIB prevention of blindness services department, 224 Great Portland Street, London W1N 6AA). They will be sent a letter giving information on what is involved, and a donor card to sign and keep.

Alternatively, all that needs to be done is to complete one of the multi-donor bequest cards available at chemists' shops, doctors' surgeries, hospitals. You should carry this card around with you, and also tell your next of kin that you wish your eyes to be used. If you go into hospital as an inpatient, you should tell the ward sister of your bequest.

After your death, the nearest eye hospital or general

hospital with an eye department must be notified immediately.

It is essential that eyes are removed within a matter of hours and someone may come from the eye hospital to take them even before the family doctor has arrived. If the death is being reported to the coroner, the eyes should not be removed without his approval.

If at the time when you die, enough eyes are already available for the eye operations then being undertaken, or you die too far away from one of the centres where eye operations are being performed or where there is an eye bank, your eyes will not be taken.

Donating your body
You can leave instructions, in writing or orally in the presence of two witnesses during the last illness, that your body shall be given for medical purposes, teaching or research before finally being buried or cremated. This enables your executors or next of kin to do so but is not legally binding on them. (On the other hand, unless you have specifically said that you do not want this to happen, your executors or next of kin can give your body for medical purposes after your death.) You can, and should, make the arrangements yourself about bequeathing your body for medical purposes, but also tell your executors and your nearest family, because they will have to act quickly after you have died.

You can write to the professor of anatomy at your nearest university medical school, or direct to HM Inspector of Anatomy at the Department of Health and Social Security, Eileen House, 80–94 Newington Cause-

way, London SE1 6EF (in Scotland, at the Scottish Home
and Health Department, St Andrew's House, Edinburgh
EH1 3DE). No forms are sent to you to sign; forms will
be sent to your next of kin or executors after your death.

No guarantee is ever given that a body will be accepted.
Medical schools in highly populated areas receive many
bequests and if a number of donors die about the same
time, some bodies may have to be refused. Another
reason for refusal by a medical school may be the cost
of transport; some medical schools do not take up
bequests from farther away than 20 to 30 miles. However,
medical schools in sparsely populated areas often find
their work hampered by lack of bodies and the form of
bequest to one medical school may allow the transfer of
the body to another school which more urgently requires
bodies for teaching and research.

Through the Department of Health you can donate
your body generally, without specifying the medical
school. The inspector of anatomy knows the requirements of all the medical schools in the country at any
one time.

When the donor dies, the inspector of anatomy in
London or the medical school should be told immediately, if possible by telephone. For the inspector of
anatomy, the number to ring is 01-703 6380 (out of office
hours, 01-407 5522).

A few questions will be put about the circumstances
of the death. The body may be refused for a number of
reasons: for instance, if it has been the subject of a post
mortem or if death followed a recent operation or is
being investigated by a coroner.

If the body is accepted, the executors or next of kin should complete and return the form sent by the Department of Health or, if the body was donated to a specific medical school outside London, by the anatomy department of the school. These forms ask the name and age of the deceased, date of death, and the address from which the body should be collected. If a special medical certificate was sent to the donor when he made the bequest, this must be completed and signed by the deceased's doctor. If the bequest is made through the inspector of anatomy, this special medical certificate (form AA4) should be sent to the inspector of anatomy at the Department of Health, together with the other form.

Soon afterwards, either the medical school to which the body has been specifically bequeathed by the donor or, in London, the Department of Health, will send an undertaker to remove the body. Before that time, the death must be registered in the usual way because the undertaker has to take away with him the registrar's disposal certificate. If the arrangement for leaving the body had been made direct with the medical school, the undertaker who comes for the body will take away with him the special medical certificate and the medical school's forms confirming the bequest which the executor or relative has to sign.

If the body is eventually to be cremated, the executor may be asked to complete and sign the statutory application form for cremation; or this may be signed by the professor of the medical school.

The family and executors need make no further arrangements: it is the responsibility of the medical school to arrange burial or cremation when the time comes. However, the next of kin, if they wish, may ask to be allowed to make arrangements themselves for a private funeral. Otherwise, the medical school arranges and pays for a simple funeral, and makes a claim for the state death grant. Unless instructions have been given by the person handing over the body that no ceremony be held, a service is conducted at the funeral by a minister or priest of the faith professed by the deceased. The medical school does not put up individual headstones. If burial or cremation in some place other than that normally used by the medical school is requested, or particularly elaborate arrangements, the extra expense must be met by the relatives or executors.

Some medical schools give no option on the method or procedure of disposal. In fact, some make it a condition that there shall be no contact later between the executors and the medical school.

—transplants

Some of the organs of the body do not die immediately and, if they are removed promptly after death, can be transplanted and continue to function. Some people have expressed a wish, either orally or in writing, that their organs should be used to save another person's life.

There are multi-donor request cards which anyone can use to indicate that the kidneys or any other parts of the body, as specified, can be taken after death for transplant purposes. These cards are available at hospitals, chemists' shops, and from general practitioners. The completed card should be carried at all times in case of sudden death, or kept in a place where it will be found quickly. Whatever wish has been expressed, the hospital cannot remove any organ unless the relatives give consent. The request for consent has to be made at a very distressing time but there is no alternative because the time for removal is so short.

The body may have to be taken to a hospital for the transplant and, unless the hospital is asked to arrange for burial, will be returned to the family for burial or cremation.

Burial in churchyards

Everyone, whether christian or not, in theory has the
right to be buried in his parish churchyard. In practice,
there may be no space left in the churchyard, and appropriate fees have to be paid. The land which is used as
a graveyard around a Church of England parish church
is administered by the incumbent (vicar or rector). Some
churches have burial grounds separated from the church
where parishioners have the right of burial, and many
old churchyards are closed for further burials.

Anyone whose permanent addresss is within the eccle-
siastical parish is entitled to be buried there, even if he
dies somewhere else. If a parish boundary is altered, the
right to burial is in the new parish. But if the new parish
has no burial ground, he retains the right to burial in the
old parish. People who have moved away to another
parish may be denied the right to be buried in the churchyard of their previous parish, even if the new parish has
no churchyard. You can ask the vicar about the right of
burial in a particular parish.

It is the incumbent (and his parochial church council)
who decides whether to allow someone who has no right
of burial in his churchyard to be buried there, and what
fee to charge. For a non-parishioner, or someone with
no connection with the parish, the charges are likely to
be higher than for a parishioner.

The charges that are payable to the incumbent, to
church officials and to the parochial church council for
funeral services and burial in Church of England parishes
are specified in the Parochial Fees Order. Under the
1982 Parochial Fees Order, the fees payable for a burial

(excluding digging charges) with a service beforehand in the parish church come to £33. (Any payment to organist, choir or other musicians is additional; so is extra heating.) The fee for burial in a churchyard without having had a service in a church of the parish beforehand is £22.

If the parish has its own gravedigger, he will dig the grave for a fee which the vicar lays down. Otherwise, the undertaker has to hire a gravedigger.

Paying a burial fee does not buy the right to choose the location of the grave in the churchyard. The vicar allots the site. Nor does the burial fee entitle you to ownership of the grave or to the exclusive right of burial in that grave.

If you want the exclusive use of a plot in a churchyard, you must apply to the diocesan registrar to reserve a grave space, by a licence called a faculty. Although a faculty gives the right to say who can be buried in the plot, the freehold of the ground continues to belong to the church. The fee charged by the diocese for a faculty depends on the amount of work involved in the petition. It takes about six weeks for a faculty to be granted. When a person dies, it is too late to get a faculty for him but his relatives could apply for a faculty to reserve the grave for other members of the family. Anyone arranging a burial in a grave reserved by a faculty must produce the faculty or other evidence which proves his right to the grave. The incumbent charges a fee for the first and each subsequent interment in a grave reserved by faculty. An additional charge is made for removing and replacing an existing headstone for subsequent interments in a grave.

On the plan of a parish churchyard, all the graves should be numbered and the vicar should keep a record of who has been buried in each grave and which graves are reserved by faculty.

The family of anyone who is buried in a churchyard is responsible for looking after the grave. The parochial church council is responsible for looking after the churchyard generally and keeping the paths and walks and unused parts tidy. When granting a faculty, some dioceses stipulate that a contribution be made towards the upkeep of the churchyard.

Neither reserving a grave by faculty nor paying a burial fee gives you the right to put up a monument or other embellishment on the grave. For this, approval must be given by the incumbent and a further fee paid. The Parochial Fees Order includes the fees for permission to put up monuments and adding an inscription to an existing monument. The incumbent's authority to give permission for monuments and inscriptions is limited: anything other than a simple headstone or inscription requires a faculty.

When permission is given to erect a monument or memorial over a non-faculty grave, this does not confer exclusive use of the grave.

Burial inside a church
Today, any rights an incumbent may have had in the past to consent to a burial inside his church building have become obsolete. Faculties to permit such burials are hardly ever granted and in urban areas burial in and under a church is prohibited by law.

Burial in cemeteries

If you want to be buried but not in a churchyard, you can be buried in a cemetery. Most cemeteries are non-denominational, and run either by a local authority or by a company. A few cemeteries are owned by a particular denomination; these are generally restricted to members of that faith. All the local authority and some privately-owned cemeteries have a section of the ground consecrated by the Church of England, and a separate section of general ground. The fee payable to a Church of England clergyman for performing a service in the consecrated part of a cemetery in his parish is £16·50 if there has not been a service in a parish church immediately before; no fee after a prior service. Some cemeteries also have ground consecrated and reserved for other specific religious denominations. In most cemeteries, any type of religious service (or none at all) can be held. Most cemeteries have a chapel which is nondenominational, and some provide a roster of clergy of different denominations.

Fees for burial in a cemetery vary widely even within the same locality. They are set by the owners, under the terms of the appropriate Acts of Parliament. Fees and regulations are usually displayed at the cemetery. If you write to the superintendents of the local cemeteries, you will be sent lists or brochures (not always very easy to follow), from which you can compare the charges and conditions. A cemetery's fee may include the services of a clergyman; some do not allow flowers to be planted or put on graves; others do not permit any monument or memorial to be put up, except over the more expensive graves or for only a limited number of years after which the cemetery authorities can remove it. Conditions or payments for maintenance are often stipulated.

In most cemeteries, there are various categories of grave. The cheapest are public (or common) graves. The person paying the interment fee has no right to say who else may or may not be buried in the grave. The graves are marked by a number; it may be possible to put up a small memorial or plaque.

In some cemeteries, no interments will take place in a common grave for a set number of years—usually 7 or 14—after the last burial, except to bury there another member of the same family. In a few cemeteries, for a small fee a grave space can be reserved for a specified period of years from the date of payment. After this, it reverts to the cemetery unless a further fee has been paid either to reserve the space for a further period or for the exclusive right to the grave on behalf of the person buried in it, so that it becomes similar to a private (or purchased) grave.

In most cemeteries, you can buy the right of exclusive burial in a particular plot, in a similar way as by a faculty granted for a grave in a churchyard. The right used to be in perpetuity, but nowadays it is more usually granted for a specific number of years—for instance, 50 or 75.

For a private grave, you get a deed of grant (sometimes referred to as a certificate of ownership), for which some cemeteries make a small charge. Keep the deed somewhere safe and make sure your family or executors know where it is. It may have to be produced in evidence before the grave can be opened for an interment. Usually the signature of the owner of the grave is required on the cemetery's application form to authorise the opening of a private grave. If the owner has died, the cemetery will probably require some alternative formality to authorise the use of the grave. Afterwards, the deed will be endorsed with details of the burial and returned to the executors. An interment fee has to be paid in addition, and also a fee for any monument, kerb, border or other embellishment that may be put up, as well as for removing and replacing an existing headstone.

Another category of grave is the so-called lawn grave, in which you have the right to exclusive burial but can put up only a very simple headstone, leaving the rest of the grave grass. These graves are always together in one part of the cemetery. You pay less for this type of grave because it is easy to keep lawn graves tidy by mowing them all together. Again, the interment fee is additional. You may not find lawn graves specified as such in a cemetery's list of charges and may have to ask whether there are any lawn graves.

On the plan of a cemetery, the various categories of grave are shown (often by different colours), and you can find from this plan which graves are available at the time.

The fees charged depend on the type, the size and the depth of the grave and, for a private or a lawn grave, also on its position (in other words, how accessible it is).

A grave which is not lined but is cut into the earth without side support is called an earth grave. A brick grave has a bricked (or concrete) floor and walls and is more expensive than an earth one. To have a brick grave, you must have the exclusive right in the grave. Some cemeteries charge a higher interment fee for a brick than for an earth grave and require longer notice for the burial. Formalities and the construction of a brick grave can take weeks. The standard size of a single grave varies slightly from cemetery to cemetery and a grave larger than the standard size costs more. What is listed as a vault is in some cemeteries a bricked double grave, in others a grave bricked right up to the level of the ground instead of to the top of the coffin.

In most local authority cemeteries, a higher fee is asked or an additional charge is made for non-residents and non-ratepayers; there may be some concessions for former residents and their relatives. Interment fees are less for children than for adults; each cemetery authority defines its own age limits. Separate charges are made by some cemetery authorities for a minister's services, music, grave maintenance.

Most local authority cemeteries have an application form which the executor or next of kin usually has to sign. All fees have to be paid in advance, and all the required documents sent to the cemetery a stipulated time before the funeral.

Each cemetery keeps a register of burials, and a record of who owns a grave plot and who has already been buried in each grave. Copies of entries in the register can be bought at any time for a small fee.

Other burial grounds
If you want to be buried in ground other than a church-yard or cemetery, the law stipulates that such private

burials must be registered. Even if you are the freeholder of the land, you must ascertain from the deeds whether the land is restricted in the use to which it may be put. If you want to bury someone in your garden, you must apply for and obtain permission from your local planning authority, and the local environmental health department must be notified and given the opportunity to object to the proposal.

FOR BURIAL—THE DOCUMENTS

registrar's certificate for burial (the disposal certificate)	from registrar	required before burial can take place	via relative and undertaker to burial authorities. Part C returns to registrar
or after inquest: coroner's order for burial	from coroner	authorises burial	
application for burial in cemetery	from cemetery via undertaker, usually signed by executor or next of kin	applies for burial and confirms arrangements	to cemetery authorities
grave deeds or faculty	from cemetery or diocese	proves right to grave	to burial authorities
copy of entry in burial register	from burial authorities	proves burial and locates grave	to executor or next of kin

No one can be cremated unless the cause of death has been definitely ascertained. This means that, unlike burial which can be carried out on the authority of a disposal certificate issued before registration, cremation cannot normally be applied for until after the death has been registered or a coroner's certificate for cremation given.

It used to be illegal to cremate the body of anyone who had left instructions that he did not wish it. Nowadays, however, there is no restriction. Even if the deceased had left specific instructions that he wanted his body to be cremated, there is no legal obligation on executors or next of kin to carry out his wishes.

People who wish to be cremated can register with the Cremation Society (Woodcut House, Ashford Road, Hollingsbourne, Maidstone, Kent ME17 1XH) under a scheme which the Society calls F.A.T.E. ('Funeral arrangements for use by trustees and executors'). The registration fee is £10. The particulars you give about yourself (doctor, next of kin, executor, solicitor, life insurance policies, whereabouts of your will, type of funeral service you would like, any bequests for medical research) are recorded and a copy sent to you, with an identity card for you to carry which asks that the Cremation Society be informed before any funeral arrangements are made on your death. (A note to executors or family on a piece of plain paper is just as valid, albeit less formal.)

The Society has also founded the Pharos Assurance Friendly Society, offering schemes for people to pay an annual premium for a sum insured towards their funeral expenses.

the formalities

Before cremation can take place, four statutory forms have to be completed, one by the next of kin, the others by three different doctors. The forms are issued by the crematorium; undertakers, as a rule, have a supply of them.

Form A is the application for cremation, and has to be completed by the executor, or next of kin, and countersigned by a householder who knows him personally.

Forms B and C and F are on the same piece of paper. B has to be completed by the doctor who attended the deceased during the last illness and who has to see the body before he can complete the form. The doctor will probably need to ask the relatives, or whoever was present at the death, for some of the information demanded on form B—for instance, whether the deceased had undergone any operation during the final illness or within a year before death; if the deceased had had a pacemaker and whether this has been removed.

Form C, the confirmatory medical certificate, has to be completed by a doctor who has been registered as a medical practitioner in the UK for at least 5 years, who must not be a relative of the deceased nor a relative or partner of the doctor who completed form B. The second doctor also has to see the body before he completes the form. Each of the doctors is entitled to a fee of £16 for the completion of the certificates, and may also charge travelling expenses. A fee of £24 may be charged for removing a pacemaker.

Forms B and C are not required when a coroner has issued a certificate for cremation. When a death is reported to the coroner, you must let him know from the outset if you want the body to be cremated, so that his authority to dispose of it will be in the form of a certificate for cremation (otherwise you may have to go back to him to get the proper certificate). In the rare cases when the coroner has reason for not allowing the body to be cremated, he will not give a certificate for cremation but will issue an order for burial instead. The next of kin must accept this, or wait until he does authorise cremation.

The final authority to cremate the body is given on form F, signed by yet another doctor, the medical referee of the crematorium. He usually does so on the basis of the medical evidence of forms B and C, or after he has received a coroner's certificate for cremation. The medical referee has the power to refuse authority to cremate, and if he cannot be fully satisfied through forms B and C, he may himself order a post mortem or refer the matter to the coroner. The relatives of the deceased have no right to prevent this. If they do not want a post mortem to be held, they will have to forgo cremation and have the body buried instead. If they agree to the post mortem, they will have to pay for it (in rare cases, the crematorium does so).

If the body of a stillborn child is to be cremated, a special medical certificate has to be completed by a doctor who was present at the stillbirth or who examined the body. No second medical certificate is required. The crematorium's medical referee has to complete his form of authority to cremate.

The purpose of all these form is to prevent any body

being cremated while there are any possible doubts about the circumstances of the death.

Most crematoria produce at least one other form on which the person organising the funeral confirms any details already provisionally arranged, such as the date and time of cremation. Some crematoria ask for specific instructions about the disposal of the ashes on this form, others have yet another form for this.

The forms have to be submitted to the medical referee of the crematorium by a stipulated time—never less than twenty-four hours—before the cremation is due. The reservation of a time for the cremation is accepted subject to the forms reaching the crematorium within the specified time limit and the fees being paid in advance.

The majority of crematoria are run by local authorities. Each crematorium has its own scale of fees and there is considerable variation between them. Some do not cremate at the weekend, others make an additional or double charge for cremation on a saturday or sunday or after normal hours. Some crematoria penalise late-comers by moving the cremation to the end of the day and charging an extra fee. Many crematoria have brochures giving details of what they offer and their charges. The fees range from about £20 to £130; for a child (depending on age) from about £5 to £42.

The charge for a cremation usually includes the fee for the medical referee's signing of form F and the use of the crematorium's chapel, whether you have a service there or not. The chapel is non-denominational. Some crematoria have a roster of chaplains of various denominations. But it is usually expected that arrangements for a clergyman, priest or minister to take a service at the crematorium will be made by the family or undertaker.

If you do not wish it, there is no need to have a religious service at the crematorium, but you should make this clear at the time of booking.

Crematoria work to a strict appointments systems, so any service has to be fairly short, unless a special booking is made for a longer period.

Recorded music in the crematorium chapel is usually included in the fee, or there may be an organ. At the time of arranging the cremation, you can ask for the organist to play a particular piece of music, but you cannot normally choose the recorded music.

Each crematorium has to keep a register of its cremations. You can get a certified copy of an entry in the register, for which a small charge is made. You are only likely to need such evidence if for some reason the death has not been registered in this country, or ashes are being sent to another country which has stringent requirements about the identity of the parcel containing the ashes.

disposal of the ashes

There is no law regulating the disposal of cremated remains. The crematorium will keep them free of charge for a limited time, usually a month. Then, in the absence of any special instructions, the ashes are either buried or scattered, whichever is the practice at the particular crematorium. The basic fee in many crematoria includes scattering or burial; otherwise this costs anything from £1·50 to £9 extra. A crematorium charges an additional fee for scattering ashes from a cremation elsewhere. If you want the crematorium to keep ashes for a period longer than the time it normally keeps them without charge, you will have to pay on a monthly basis.

A crematorium scatters or buries ashes in what it calls its garden of remembrance. The ground there is usually not consecrated and the place is not marked. The deceased's family can ask to witness the proceedings (some crematoria charge a fee), but there is generally no formal ceremony.

If a relative wants to take away the ashes, they can be collected from the crematorium about 24 hours after the cremation, in a container for which a charge is made. For a similar charge (plus postage), the crematorium will post the ashes to the person who applied for the cremation. Because the ashes are in the form of very fine powder, they are usually sealed in a polythene bag inside the container, to prevent any escaping.

The undertaker may be willing to collect and keep the ashes until they are to be disposed of. The person taking away the ashes usually has to sign a receipt for them and may be asked to state how they will be finally disposed of.

With the ashes, the crematorium gives or sends a certificate which confirms that the cremation has taken place. This certificate, which is usually free, will be required by the church or cemetery authorities where the ashes are going to be buried or scattered.

Ashes can be scattered, anywhere, provided it is not done too flamboyantly or carelessly. The Church of England has certain stipulations about the disposal of ashes in consecrated ground: direct committal into the earth is preferred, strewing or scattering is discouraged.

Ashes can be buried in most churchyards and cemeteries. Some have a separate section for this. The interment fee for burying ashes in a churchyard is similar to that for a body, in a cemetery less. Burial of ashes is sometimes permitted in a churchyard which has had to be closed for ordinary burials, but a faculty may be required.

Usually, ashes are funnelled direct into the ground. You may be allowed to set a small plaque into the ground or nearby wall to mark the place in the churchyard where the ashes were put. Some churches keep a book of remembrance inside the church; a charge of a few pounds is made for an entry in this.

FOR CREMATION—THE DOCUMENTS

registrar's certificate for cremation (the disposal certificate) or	from registrar	required before cremation can be applied for	via relative and undertaker to crematorium authorities. Part C returns to registrar
after post mortem or inquest: coroner's certificate for cremation	from coroner	authorises disposal of body (supersedes forms B and C)	
form A	from crematorium via undertaker, to be completed by executor or next of kin	applies for cremation and confirms arrangements	to crematorium authorities
form B	from crematorium via undertaker, to be completed by deceased's doctor	certifies cause of death	to medical referee at crematorium

form C	from crematorium via undertaker, to be completed by a second doctor	confirms cause of death in form B	to medical referee at crematorium
form F	from crematorium, to be completed by medical referee	authorises cremation	kept by crematorium authorities
form —	from crematorium via undertaker, to be completed by executor or next of kin	confirms arrangements; gives instructions for disposal of ashes	to crematorium authorities
certificate for disposal of cremated remains (for burial)	from crematorium	confirms cremation and gives details of the death	via relatives to burial authorities
certificate of cremation	from crematorium	copy of entry in register	to executor or next of kin

THE FUNERAL

Whether the body is to be buried or cremated, many of the arrangements can be made by an individual on his own. But it is rare for a funeral to be carried out without the services of an undertaker.

Undertakers
The trade of undertaking started as a comprehensive business some 200 years ago when, in towns, some carpenters began to specialise in the production of coffins and some carriage proprietors in providing funeral carriages. Gradually, these functions merged and developed until the 'undertaking' of a funeral and its arrangements became a separate trade. Some firms of undertakers subcontract by hiring hearse, cars, and bearers.

The status of undertakers was strengthened in the victorian era by the fashion for elaborate, often ostentatious, funerals. More recently, undertakers adopted the title of funeral director and formed the National Association of Funeral Directors (57 Doughty Street, London WC1N 2NE). Members of the NAFD undertake to observe a code of practice drawn up in consultation with the Office of Fair Trading. This includes giving full information about services and prices, providing a written estimate of all charges and a detailed account, offering a basic simple funeral if required. The code also covers general and professional conduct, including confidentiality and the procedure for complaints.

The undertaker's purpose is to assume total responsibility for organising and supplying the necessities for a funeral. The transaction is a business deal and, even though it may be difficult for the next of kin or executor to be businesslike in the circumstances, it should be treated as such, hard-hearted though it may seem.

It is not part of an executor's formal duty to be responsible for arranging the funeral. The family should agree who is to be in charge of and supervise the arrangements.

Arrangements for the funeral can be made but should not be confirmed before the disposal certificate from the registrar or coroner is available, to be given to the undertaker.

At the time of asking an undertaker to quote, you should have a fairly clear idea of what kind of funeral is wanted and how much can be spent on it. Some people insure during their lifetime for their funeral, or join one of the special friendly societies which pay out a lump sum on death. An undertaker may ask whether the deceased was insured in this way; he then has a better idea of how much the funeral should come to. But usually the cost of a funeral is paid out of the deceased's estate—the money and property he left.

If you intend to spend no more than a limited sum, tell the undertaker and ask what he is prepared to provide for that figure. Do not be persuaded into anything you do not really want, even if he assures you that everyone else has this or that. The undertaker is in business and is justified in trying to sell as many of his services as he can.

You can have preliminary discussions with the undertaker on the telephone, but to conclude the arrangements, he generally comes to you or you have to go to his office. Wherever you see him, the undertaker should show you a price list for the types of funeral he can provide. Ask for a little time on your own to study this and perhaps discuss alternatives with the family and decide what extras you want him to organise by way of transport, flowers, notices, catering.

In many cases, the member of the undertaker's staff with whom you have the first interview remains in charge for the whole funeral. One of the first things he will want to know is where the body is and whether it is to remain there. If there has been a post mortem, you must get the undertaker to fetch the body from the mortuary. If he has to send someone to lay out or take away a body in the middle of the night or at the weekend, he will charge extra.

If the body is to remain in the house rather than await the funeral at the undertaker's, he will arrange for it to be laid out if the nurse or any member of the family has not already done so. A nurse refers to laying out as the 'last offices', the undertaker calls it the 'first offices'. If the undertaker takes the body away without having laid it out, he will want to know what to do with clothing, and any jewellery, that he takes off the body and will ask what he should dress the body in—shroud or robe, or the deceased's own nightwear.

When he comes to collect a body from the house or a hospital, the undertaker uses either a covered stretcher or a form of coffin which is called a shell. He takes the body away in a small hearse, in an ambulance, or in an anonymous-looking van known in the trade as a handy. In order to remove a body from a hospital, the undertaker usually has to have some written authority, such as the disposal certificate or an authorisation form signed by an executor or relative.

Most undertakers will keep the body on their premises until the time of the funeral. Usually relatives (and, with their permission, friends) can go to see the body in what is variously called a chapel of rest, reposing room or slumber room. With some undertakers, you have to make an appointment beforehand. Some undertakers also have their own chapel for private prayer in which a religious service can be held at the beginning of the funeral, before going to the cemetery or crematorium.

embalming
Because it is easier to deal with a body when it has been embalmed, most undertakers like to embalm the body and some insist on doing so. They are likely to call it preservative or hygienic treatment. If you do not want the body to be embalmed, tell the undertakers, because they generally embalm any body brought to their premises without specifically asking the family about it.

Before a body is embalmed, the doctor must have given his medical certificate of cause of death, and it would be unwise to embalm until a disposal certificate has been given. If the death is reported to the coroner, the body must not be embalmed until he has given his authority. If the body is to be cremated, the two doctors must have completed the forms for cremation before the body is embalmed.

Embalming, which is intended to delay the process of decomposition, involves replacing blood with a solution of formalin and other chemicals. It is temporary and is not comparable to the ancient egyptian process of mummification. In this country, embalmers tend not to use cosmetics, but try to create an appearance of sleep. A body can be embalmed at home, but usually the embalming is done at the undertaker's.

In a mortuary, the bodies are kept refrigerated, and some undertakers, too, use this method of preservation instead of embalming. When relatives then come to see the body, it is brought from the cold room to the undertaker's chapel or to one of the reposing, slumber or rest rooms.

Funeral costs

NAFD undertakers all have to offer what is called a basic simple funeral. This includes only the bare minimum. It is as well to be aware of what services the undertaker is supplying for the stated price, and how much any additional items would cost. Different firms include different items in their inclusive charge, but all will include a coffin, a hearse and one following car up to a stated mileage, the bearers to carry the coffin, the services of an undertaker. There is no breakdown given of the cost of these services, which each undertaker assesses according to his own overheads and profit margin. The lowest prices quoted by undertakers for a simple inclusive funeral start at not much less than £250.

The price quoted for a complete funeral is based on the type of coffin. If you choose one of the undertaker's more expensive coffins, you will get a more elaborate standard of funeral. The undertaker should be able to show you illustrations of the different coffins and caskets he can supply. A casket is rectangular, instead of the traditional tapered shape of a coffin; it is usually more expensive than a coffin. The wood affects the price: veneered chipboard is cheapest and japanese oak the most expensive.

The linings of coffins, and other fittings such as pillows and handles, vary considerably according to the price of the coffin. Handles can be expensive, especially if made of brass, and are in many cases ornamental and not used for carrying the coffin (except at jewish funerals). Many undertakers buy plain coffins from a wholesaler or coffin-maker and keep their own stock of handles, linings and other fittings, which they fix to each coffin when it is ordered. A nameplate will be put on the coffin when the body is in it, giving the name, the date of death and the age of the deceased.

In victorian and edwardian days, it was the practice of the upper classes to use a kind of double coffin, the inner one being a lighter cloth-finished version of the solid, more elaborate outer one. The first cremation coffins were replicas of these inner ones. When an outer coffin was also used at a cremation, the inner case was taken out and the body cremated in it; the outer coffin was not burned (and was sometimes used again).

Nowadays for cremation it is usual to have a simple and unadorned coffin, with handles and fittings not made of metal. It should therefore be at the cheap end of the price range. It is sometimes covered with a pall throughout the funeral.

A funeral often involves costs not covered by the undertaker's price for a basic funeral: laying out the body, removing the body from the house or hospital to the undertaker's (extra if the removal has to be done outside normal working hours), a shroud or robe, extra cars and additional mileage if the hearse or cars have to go beyond the undertaker's mileage limit. If he does an extra journey—to take the coffin to a church the night before the funeral, for example, or to fetch the body from the mortuary after a post mortem—there will be an extra charge.

Undertakers ought to be able to tell you charges and conditions of the different churches, cemeteries and crematoria in the area. When comparing the scales of charges in the district, remember that undertakers' charges increase with the distance the funeral has to go.

All undertakers who are NAFD members must give an itemised written estimate of costs, and most will provide a formal confirmation of funeral arrangements. Even if you 'leave it to him', you should get from him an estimate of the likely cost and what later additions (for instance, extra cars) will cost. Tell the undertaker not to incur such expenses without your authorisation—funeral guests may ask him to drive them to the railway station twelve miles away, or the clergyman request to be picked up or taken home by car.

Church, cemetery or cremation fees have to be paid on top of the undertaker's charge, as do all other payments such as fees for clergyman and organist.

Generally, the total cost of a funeral, including burial or cremation fees, is unlikely to come to less than about £400, and can be much more. The price levels vary between different parts of the country (for instance, prices tend to be higher in London and the south), as well as varying between local firms.

Which? November 1982 includes a report on funerals.

—stillbirths

A stillborn child does not usually have a funeral, but an undertaker will arrange the disposal of a stillborn child without any ceremony, for an inclusive charge. The hospital or midwife may offer to have arrangements made on the parents' behalf, free of charge.

Final arrangements

The undertaker must have the registrar's disposal certificate (or the coroner's equivalent authorisation) before confirming the final arrangements. He will see to it that all official forms are completed and taken to the right people at the right time. For a burial, for instance, he takes charge of any grave deeds and gets a cemetery's form of application signed by the executor. For a cremation, he sees that a relative or the executor completes the form of application and the form giving instructions for disposal of the ashes. He will also arrange for two doctors to complete forms B and C and pay out their fees and, when he has gathered the necessary forms, he will get them to the medical referee at the crematorium in time.

The fees to the vicar, sexton, gravedigger, organist, choirmaster, chaplain and officials at the cemetery or crematorium, as the case may be, usually have to be paid in advance. The undertaker will make the actual payments and will add the charges to his total account.

In effect, the undertaker should co-ordinate the various operations at the different stages. He will approach the people in charge of wherever it has been decided the burial or cremation is to take place (this usually means the local clergyman or superintendent of the cemetery or crematorium) in order to reserve a time and, for a burial, to order the type of grave you want. He can also be asked to make the arrangements for whatever service is to be held. Either the undertaker or a member of the family should ask whoever the family wants to officiate at any service, whether he is willing to do so and whether he will be available at the time planned for holding the ceremony.

Most religious denominations have some form of funeral ceremony. In this country, unless the dead person had professed another religion, the Church of England service will probably be said at his funeral. Rituals can be adapted according to the preferences of those concerned. For instance, the main part of the service can be said in the church or at the undertaker's with only a few words of committal at the graveside, or all the service can be at the grave. A funeral address may be given either in the church or outside, or not at all. A service in a crematorium or cemetery chapel is restricted by the time allowed—normally less than half an hour.

Anyone who specifically does not want any form of religious service must make this very clear to whoever is going to make the funeral arrangements. Although not customary, there is no reason why a body cannot be buried or cremated without any form of religious ceremony. If a body is to be buried in a churchyard without a religious ceremony (or with one, but held by a minister of another denomination), the incumbent of the parish is supposed to be given forty-eight hours' notice in writing. In practice, most vicars would give permission if asked over the telephone. The usual parish regulations apply and fees have to be paid.

If there is to be no service at a cemetery or crematorium, all that needs to be done is to arrange with the authorities the day and time of the funeral. Most cemeteries permit a non-religious ceremony to be held at the graveside, provided this is done in a reasonably dignified way. The British Humanist Association (13 Prince of Wales Terrace, London W8 5PG) may be able to send someone to officiate at a humanist funeral ceremony or will send a booklet (£1·50) detailing the procedure that could be followed. The South Place Ethical Society (Conway Hall, Red Lion Square, London WC1R 4RL) can provide notes and suggested text for a funeral ceremony, or the names of appropriate officiants. The Rationalist Press Association (88 Islington High Street, London N1 8EW) and the National Secular Society (702 Holloway Road, London N19 3NL) would be able to arrange for someone to take a service in the London area, and in a few places in other parts of the country. A fee or a donation will be expected, and the officiant's expenses paid. The Humanist Funeral Officiators (32 Over Street, Brighton, East Sussex) can generally send someone to conduct a service in most parts of south east England.

Denominational burial grounds usually insist on their own form of service. If you are involved in arranging the funeral of someone of a faith different from your own, get in touch as soon as possible with the equivalent of the local parish priest of that denomination, to find out what needs to be done. With orthodox jews, for example, the body should be buried as soon as possible once the disposal certificate is issued. If a man subscribes to a synagogue burial society, he or his wife or his dependent children will be buried, free, by the society in its cemetery. The funeral and coffin will be very simple, and there will be no flowers. Orthodox jews do not get cremated, and embalming or bequeathing a body for medical purposes is not allowed. Non-orthodox jews are more flexible and there is less difference between their funerals and those of other denominations. The funeral will always be simple, but flowers are allowed and so is cremation. Not all non-orthodox synagogues have a subscription system for their burial society; with those who do not, the cost of the funeral is paid by the family. A synagogue sometimes agrees that its burial society may carry out the funeral of a jew who was not an active member of a synagogue and had not been subscribing to any burial society, but his family will be charged for the funeral and the cost will be considerably more. There is rarely any difference between the funeral of members of the same synagogue; all are simple. If a jew dies when away from home, it is the responsibility and expense of the relatives to bring the body back for the synagogue burial society to take over.

For a practising roman catholic, it is usual to arrange for the priest to say a requiem mass in the local parish church. There are no set fees laid down for roman catholic priests to charge for funeral services, but it is usual for the deceased's family to make an offering to the church. Cremation is no longer discouraged for roman catholics, and crematoria have roman catholic priests on their roster.

Notices

Announcements of deaths are usually made in the national and local newspapers most likely to be read by the deceased's friends and acquaintances. Many newspapers, including the national dailies, will accept the text by telephone, provided the office can telephone back to read over to a member of the family or the undertaker the text that is going to be printed. The papers do not usually ask for evidence that the death has occurred, unless the notice is submitted by someone who is not a relative or executor or the undertaker. When the undertaker inserts the notice on behalf of his client, he may ask if he should include his firm's name and address, usually as being able to supply more information about the funeral or to receive flowers beforehand. The cost of an announcement will be based on the number of lines the notice comes to.

The national daily newspapers insist on a standard form of announcement: the family name of the dead person, the date of death and the place (the cause of death is not usually included, nor are the names of hospitals), the deceased's full name (but the papers exercise their editorial control strictly, even to the extent of excising nicknames), home address and often some mention of the remaining family.

Details of time, date and place of the funeral can be included. Anyone who has not been specifically invited but wishing to attend is expected to arrive independently at the time and place announced in the press. If the family wants to restrict attendance at the funeral, the notice should say 'funeral private'. When a funeral is announced as private, only those whom the family has asked to come should attend. If the relatives think that a great many people might wish to come, they may arrange for the funeral to be private followed by a memorial service some days or weeks later for all those who wish to pay tribute to the dead person. If no details of the time and place of the funeral are published at all, it is to be assumed that the funeral is to be a private one.

Flowers

The notice in the newspaper should also make it clear if no flowers are wanted (or no letters). Sometimes only the family's, or only certain types of flowers are requested.

A 'no flowers' request should be strictly observed. Sometimes other ways are suggested in which sympathy can be expressed: for example, by giving plants or shrubs to the cemetery or crematorium garden, or, more usually, by donations in the name of the deceased to a particular charity or organisation in which he or she was interested.

For flowers, the newspaper notice should specifically state where they are to be sent. If the flowers go to the undertaker (or direct to the cemetery or crematorium), it is important that the deceased's name should be clearly stated on the label. The undertaker can be asked to make a list of the people who have sent flowers, so that the next of kin have a record afterwards. He will transport the flowers with the coffin to the church, cemetery or crematorium. When the body is buried, the flowers are left on or near the grave. A crematorium may restrict where flowers can be put and reserve the right to dispose of flowers afterwards.

The funeral
You can arrange with the undertaker that the funeral
shall start from your home or from his premises, usually
depending on where the body is. Or you can ask him to
take the body direct to the church, cemetery or crematorium for mourners to meet there. If the undertaker
provides cars for the family and other special mourners,
he will marshal the cortege and arrange when it shall
start. Timing is important because the cemetery or crematorium authorities may add to, or even double, their
charge if the funeral arrives late.

You should discuss and make a clear arrangement with
the undertaker beforehand about the procedure at the
end of the funeral—for instance, whether you want him
to take people home—and at what point you will not
need him any more.

Before the undertaker closes the lid of the coffin, he
may ask the relatives or executors if they would like to
witness this and see the body again (euphemistically, to
pay their last respects). This also acts as a safeguard to
check the identity of the body before finally closing the
coffin.

—burial
At a burial preceded by a church service, the coffin is
taken into the church by the bearers and placed in front
of the altar. The mourners normally follow the coffin.
In some anglican as well as roman catholic churches, the
coffin may be taken into the church the previous evening,
and remains there before the altar until the service. After
the service, the bearers take the coffin from the church

to the grave while the mourners follow, led there by a member of the graveyard or cemetery staff. If the service has been held elsewhere, or there is no service, the coffin is carried direct from the hearse to the grave.

At some more formal funerals, there are pall bearers who walk alongside the coffin but do not carry anything. Originally, they used to carry the pall, a heavy canopy which was held over the coffin. Nowadays, a form of pall is sometimes laid on top of a coffin to cover it during the service.

The bearers lower the coffin into the grave, on webbing slings, while the words of committal are said. The mourners sometimes throw earth on to the coffin, but they usually do not stay to see the complete filling-in of the grave, which is done later by the cemetery or graveyard staff.

Burying ashes in a churchyard or cemetery can be done with as much or as little ceremony as the relatives wish, by arrangement with the incumbent of the parish or with the superintendent of the cemetery.

—cremation

Before a cremation, either the service takes place in a church with the words of committal said at the crematorium chapel, or the whole service is held at the crematorium. The coffin is taken into the crematorium chapel, followed by the mourners, and laid on the catafalque. As the committal sentences are being said, the coffin passes out of sight, by being lowered or moved mechanically through a door, or by a curtain being drawn across it. You may be given an option for this not to happen until everyone has left the chapel, and in some crematoria there is no provision for removing the coffin during the service so that the mourners leave while the coffin is still in the chapel. The coffin goes into the committal room, to await cremation. If no religious service is being held, the coffin may pass straight into the committal room. The body is not taken out of the coffin, and each coffin is burnt individually in a cremator (which is what the special type of furnace is called).

The executors or next of kin can, when making arrangements for the cremation, ask to be allowed to go into the committal room to see the coffin placed in the cremator. Usually only two people are allowed.

After about an hour to one and a half hours, the ashes are taken from the cremator. If the ashes are not left to be scattered or buried at the crematorium, you can ask the undertaker to collect them and post or give them to you. Most undertakers offer a selection of urns or special boxes for you to put the ashes in. Or an undertaker will, for a fee, scatter the ashes for you in a suitable part of a park or garden. Some undertakers will, also for a fee, keep ashes until the time when they can be mingled with the ashes of, say, the husband or wife, to be scattered or buried together.

Arrangements such as these do not need to be made at the funeral. You can see the undertaker later.

—afterwards

After the funeral, light refreshments are sometimes provided for the mourners, usually in the house of a member of the immediate family, or the undertaker may make arrangements at a local restaurant. In the days when attending a funeral involved a lengthy journey and considerable time, a substantial meal used to be provided afterwards. Nowadays, this rarely happens.

The undertaker will send in his account fairly soon after the funeral. He is likely to offer a discount of 5 per cent or 10 per cent for full payment within a stipulated time—say, two or four weeks.

The undertaker's account should be as detailed as possible, and show separately what is due to him for his services and the coffin, and what he has paid out on your behalf (where possible, with receipted bills): the burial or cremation charges, doctors' fees, and any other payments he made, such as the cost of any flowers you asked him to order. This will enable you to check that no tips or other extras were paid out except those you had specifically requested him to give. Tips to bearers, grave diggers, cemetery or crematorium staff could mount up considerably.

However, many of the payments that the undertaker will have made for you are expenses you would have incurred anyway. He may have inserted a notice in the newspaper on your behalf, or arranged catering for the funeral, or ordered special stationery.

The undertaker's charges for the funeral, including the supply of a coffin, shroud or a robe, are exempt from value added tax, and so is the fee for burial or cremation, and any fee paid to a clergyman for conducting the funeral service. For any goods or services concerned with the commemoration of the dead—for example, a headstone, plant, entry in a book of remembrance—value added tax has to be paid. Obituary notices in newspapers are zero-rated, but VAT has to be paid on charges for flowers and for catering.

Memorials

A headstone or other memorial in a churchyard or cemetery is subject to the restrictions imposed by the church or by the cemetery. There will be stipulations affecting the size, shape and material of any memorial and the words and lettering of an inscription. Many burial grounds and nearly all churchyards nowadays prohibit kerbs or surrounds to graves, and memorials are usually restricted to a headstone, plinth and vase set at the head of the grave.

The family or the monumental mason must apply to the church or cemetery authorities for permission to do anything to mark the grave. A copy of the entry in the burial register may be asked for or, if the grave is a private or faculty one, whoever is applying has to produce the deeds as authorisation and as a means of identifying the grave. The undertaker is not usually involved in these arrangements but he should warn you of any restrictions he knows about memorials when you are choosing between burial grounds. Some undertakers run a firm of monumental masons in addition to their undertaking business.

Normally, a headstone cannot be erected or replaced after a second burial until the ground has settled over the grave, usually several months after the burial. Less reputable monumental masons, on finding out when a funeral is being held, importune the family with discreditable haste, even at the graveside or by calling at the house on the day of the funeral. Do not yield to their persistence and persuasiveness.

To get the names of established local firms of monumental masons, you can write to the National Association of Master Masons (Admin House, Market Square (north side), Leighton Buzzard, Beds LU7 7EU) for a list of their members in the locality.

You should not commission a monumental mason to carry out any work for you without knowing what the burial ground's regulations are. The mason should be able to advise you on these, and show you in his brochure or display area the various types of memorial that would be suitable. The cost depends on the material—stone, marble, granite—and the size, ornamentation and finish.

Written permission must be obtained from the church or cemetery authorities for what is proposed. In a churchyard, this may necessitate a faculty and the wording of an inscription must be approved in writing by the incumbent; most parishes object to colloquialism and informal descriptions such as 'grandad', and generally stipulate that any quotations are from the bible.

A fee for the privilege of erecting a memorial has to be paid to the church or cemetery authorities. It is usually paid by the mason and charged to the client on the final account. This fee is exempt from value added tax.

Before ordering a memorial, ask for a written estimate clearly stating the items and total cost, including any delivery or erection charges, value added tax and the church or cemetery fees. Value added tax is charged on the cost of adding an inscription to an existing stone and on a new headstone, but not on the removal and replacement of an existing memorial. It is usual for masons to ask for a 10 per cent deposit to be paid by the client when confirming the order for a memorial.

—after cremation

About a week after the cremation, the crematorium will probably send a brochure telling you what memorials are offered, with prices (value added tax is chargeable on these). These are optional extras—there is no need to have them.

Hand-lettered inscriptions in the book of remembrance, which is kept at the crematorium, usually consist of the name, date of death and a short epitaph. The charge depends on the length of the entry. The crematorium displays the book open at the right page on the anniversary of the death (not of the date of cremation) for a limited number of years. Some crematoria sell a miniature reproduction of the entry in the book of remembrance, in the form of a card or bound as a booklet. The price of the booklet depends mainly on the luxury of the binding.

The charges for the erection of memorial plaques or for inscriptions on panels in cloisters or memorial halls vary between crematoria. A number of local authority crematoria, however, allow no memorials other than an entry in the book of remembrance.

In some crematoria, there is a cloister or colonnade, called a columbarium, full of niches. The ashes are either walled in by a plaque or left in an urn in the niche. The charge for renting or buying a niche is high, and in some of the columbaria there are no more spaces left.

Some crematoria allow trees, or more usually rose-bushes, to be planted over the spot where ashes are buried or scattered, or allow plaques or memorial seats to be put in the gardens. Again, costs vary, as does the length of time for which the crematorium will see to the maintenance.

Apart from the gardens of remembrance at crematoria, there are privately-run gardens exclusively for the burial of ashes where a plot can be bought in perpetuity. The cost of a plot is not less than £500, and may be much more (and VAT is payable).

Pre-death arrangements
If you want to make the arrangements personally for your own funeral, you can approach an undertaker at any time and discuss with him what you want to happen when you die. He will refer to this as an NYD ('not yet dead') funeral and will file all the details you have agreed until the time comes to implement your directions. He may suggest that you sign a list of agreed arrangements and give a copy to your next of kin or executor. You can pay in advance towards the expenses but if costs rise in the meantime, the undertaker will claim from your estate any additional amount which is due to increased costs. If you pay in advance, it is the undertaker who gets the benefit of the interest on your money.

CHARTS

of what to do when someone dies

80

CHART 1

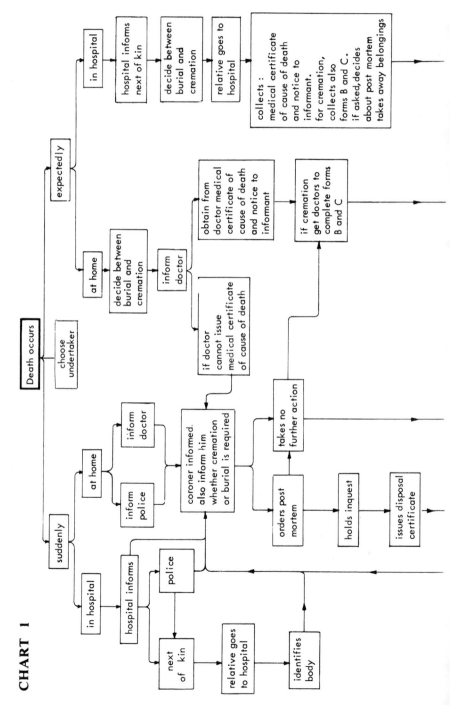

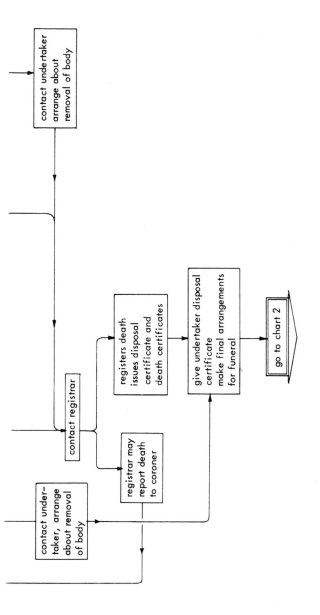

CHART 2

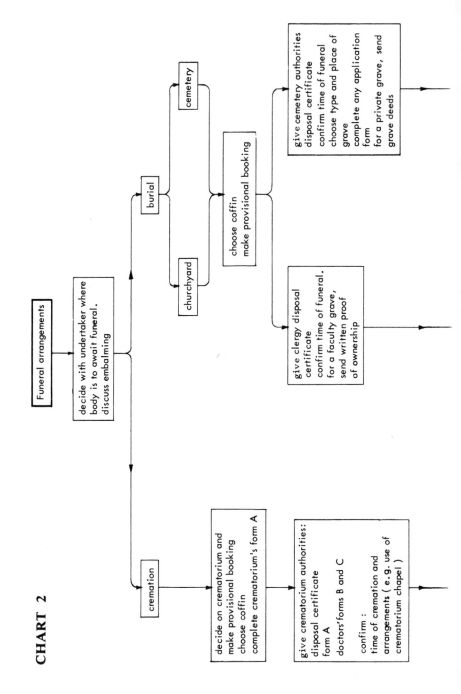

Funeral arrangements

decide with undertaker where body is to await funeral. discuss embalming

cremation

burial

churchyard · cemetery

decide on crematorium and make provisional booking choose coffin complete crematorium's form A

choose coffin make provisional booking

give crematorium authorities:
disposal certificate
form A
doctors'forms B and C

confirm:
time of cremation and arrangements (e.g. use of crematorium chapel)

give clergy disposal certificate
confirm time of funeral.
for a faculty grave, send written proof of ownership

give cemetery authorities
disposal certificate
confirm time of funeral
choose type and place of grave
complete any application form
for a private grave, send grave deeds

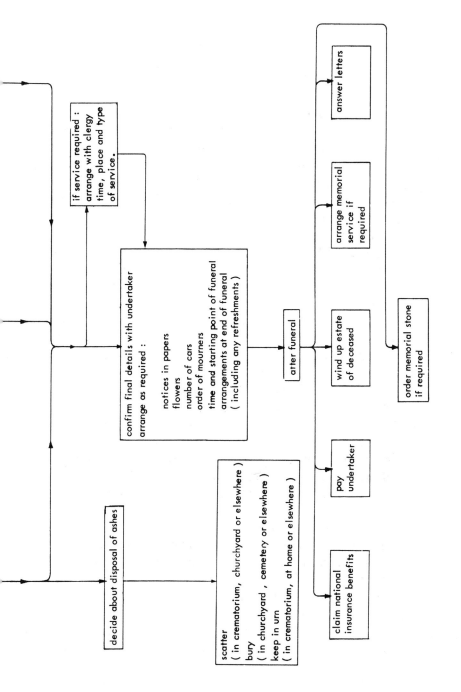

Funerals away
Some people express a wish to be buried near their family
although they now live somewhere else. If this is so, or
if someone dies in an area other than where he lived,
funeral arrangements have to be made in two places.
One undertaker will probably cope. If it is too far for
him to supervise both ends himself, he may subcontract
arrangements at the other end to a colleague, but his
contract with the other undertaker is not your concern.
Alternatively, you can contact an undertaker in the
district to which the body is to be taken and deal with
him direct.

A body is sent by road in a hearse whenever possible
because this is likely to be a quicker and cheaper means
of transport. For long distances, it may be better to send
it by rail or air, but you then have to pay for a hearse
at both ends of the journey. The charge for sending a
coffin by rail varies according to the particular route
required: the station manager can advise. The coffin
travels in a locked container, usually in the guard's van.
With the body must be sent the disposal certificate and
other documents such as grave deeds. It is usual to
embalm the body before sending it on its journey.

Sending a body abroad
Cremated remains can be sent anywhere without restrictions, and no official notice has to be given or permission
sought when ashes are being taken out of the country.
Restrictions may, however, be imposed by the authorities
at the other end.

But if the body of someone who has died in England
or Wales is going to be buried or cremated in another

country (including Scotland, Northern Ireland and the Channel Islands), the coroner of the district in which the body is lying must be told. Form 104 gives 'notice to a coroner of intention to remove a body out of England'. You can get this from the registrar when registering the death, and ask him for the name and address of the coroner to whom it should be sent. If he knows in time that the body is going out of the country, the registrar will not issue a disposal certificate. If, however, a disposal certificate has already been given, it must be sent to the coroner when sending him form 104.

The coroner gives a formal acknowledgment of this notice. The body must not then be taken out of the coroner's area for four days. Provided the coroner does not in the meantime requisition the body for a post mortem or inquest, you can go ahead with your plans for removing the body once the four days from the date of the coroner's acknowledgment are up. The coroner can waive the four-day waiting period by specifically stating this in his acknowledgment. He may do so, for instance, at the request of the executor or next of kin, if for any good reason there is urgent need to move the body out of the country by a particular date.

An undertaker will make arrangements about moving the body with British Rail, any freight-carrying airline or any shipping line. Transporting a body can be expensive. Some airlines charge twice the normal cargo rate for a body in a coffin. There may be special requirements: for example, that the coffin is enclosed in a crate or that it is airtight. Most airlines insist on the body being embalmed. This requires specially thorough embalming, and a certificate of embalming must accompany the body.

Also, the necessary freight documents must be completed. The consular office of the country to which the body is going will know what regulations have to be met. You will need one standard form of death certificate for the UK customs, and another one, or more, depending on the requirements of the country to which the body is going. You may have to have all documents translated and authenticated at the consulate of the country concerned, for which you will have to pay. The consulate will also tell you what arrangements you can make beforehand and what formalities will be required on arrival of the body.

Burying a body in the sea is removal out of England or Wales, and the coroner must be informed accordingly and his acknowledgment of the notice of intended removal obtained.

Permission has to be obtained from the local district inspector of fisheries (addresses available from the Fisheries Inspectorate, MAFF, Great Westminster House, Horseferry Road, London SW1P 2AE). Permission may not be granted along certain stretches of the coast.

The fisheries inspector should be able to suggest a suitable ship whose master knows the local tides and coast and will advise on a position least likely to yield up the body once it has been committed. The cost is a matter of bargaining between you and the master of the vessel from which the body is to be lowered. If a coffin is used, it needs to be weighted and have holes bored in it to make sure that it sinks.

If the body has been cremated, however, the ashes can be scattered on to the sea anywhere, from a boat or the beach.

Bringing a body from abroad

When a british subject dies abroad, whether as a resident there or as a visitor, his death must be registered according to local requirements and regulations. The british consul in that country can also register the death. The advantage of the death being registered by a british consul is that certified copies of the entry of death can eventually be obtained from the General Register Office in London, just as if the death had been registered here in the normal way. Otherwise there is no official record in this country of the death.

If you want to get back to this country the body of a person who died abroad, you should ask the advice of the british consul there, or of the Foreign Office consular department in London. Some of the larger firms of undertakers have agents abroad and can arrange either to have a funeral in the other country or to bring the body back here. Bringing a body back is likely to cost several hundred pounds. If the body is brought back, the UK customs require some evidence of the death to come with the body, such as a death certificate issued in the place where death occurred, or some official authorisation to remove the body issued by a local coroner (or equivalent).

Anyone arranging the funeral in England or Wales of someone who has died elsewhere, including Scotland and Northern Ireland, must supply the registrar of the district in which the body is to be buried or cremated with evidence that the death took place outside England or Wales. This evidence is either the british consul's authentication of a foreign death certificate or, if the death took place in Scotland or Northern Ireland, a death certificate issued there. The registrar of the district in England or Wales can then issue a certificate called the 'certificate of no liability to register'. This takes the place of the disposal certificate.

The coroner will be required to hold an inquest if the death was not due to a natural cause. You should allow time for the post mortem and preliminary examinations when arranging the date of the funeral.

The body must be buried within a fortnight because part of this certificate of no liability to register must be returned within fourteen days to the registrar who issued it. If a body brought from outside the UK is to be cremated, a doctor's statement of the medical cause of death must be sent with it (this may have to be translated and authenticated). You or the undertaker should send or take the completed cremation application form A and all the documents which came with the body to the Home Office, E4 division, 50 Queen Anne's Gate, London SW1H 9AT. It is wise to telephone beforehand to check that you have all the necessary documents: the telephone number is 01-213 7006 or 3044. If you post them, put 'cremation urgent' on the envelope. The Home Office then issues a certificate to take the place of forms B and C for the crematorium's medical referee.

REMOVAL TO OR FROM OTHER COUNTRIES
THE DOCUMENTS

form 104 (notice to a coroner of intention to move a body out of England)	from registrar, to be completed by executor or next of kin	gives notice that body will be taken out of country	to coroner of place where body is
coroner's acknowledg-ment of removal notice	from coroner	confirms that body may be removed after four days	to executor or next of kin, to send with body
if death abroad; certificate of no liability to register	from registrar		
part A	to be completed by relative	declares details of death and applies for part B	to registrar
part B	to be completed by registrar	states that death is not required to be registered; takes place of disposal certificate	to person who com-pleted part A
part C	to be completed by burial or cremation authorities	confirms that burial or cremation has taken place	to registrar (within 14 days) who issued part B

When someone dies on a foreign ship or aircraft, it counts as a death abroad. On a british-registered ship or aircraft, the death is recorded in the captain's log for the day. Eventually, a copy of the log entry can be obtained from the General Register Office in London.

If a member of the forces dies serving abroad, the Ministry of Defence arranges and pays for his funeral there. (In some circumstances, two close relatives may be enabled to attend.) Or it may be possible to fly the body home; once it has reached the undertaker in this country, the family becomes responsible for the funeral. The Ministry of Defence contributes a grant of £295, or £155 and a coffin. In some countries, the Ministry can arrange cremation if requested, and for the ashes to be sent home.

If a serviceman dies in this country, his funeral also will be arranged and paid for by the Ministry of Defence. Burial takes place in a military cemetery only if there is one near to where the death occurred or for some reason burial there is desirable. Cremation can be arranged if requested. If the relatives prefer to arrange the funeral themselves, they will get the Ministry grant towards this.

If someone who was receiving a war disablement pension dies as a result of that disablement, the Department of Health and Social Security may arrange and pay for a simple funeral. The next of kin should contact the local war pensions office straightaway. Alternatively, the Department will make a grant equivalent to the full death grant for any such pensioner if he does not qualify for the full state death grant.

Local authority funerals

When someone dies who has either no relatives or none able or willing to pay for the funeral, the hospital or the local authority of the area where the person died or where the body was found has to arrange the funeral, and if necessary to pay the costs. If the police have a body in their charge for which they cannot trace any relative, they notify the local authority who then has to arrange the funeral.

No arrangements should be made by anyone with an undertaker before getting in touch with the local authority social services department or the district health authority. Most local authorities and health authorities have a contract with a local undertaker for a very simple funeral. The relevant authority claims any state death grant that may be payable.

Cases of hardship

Where someone entitled to supplementary benefit is responsible for arranging the funeral of a person who was ordinarily resident in Great Britain, but cannot afford to pay for it, some of the cost can be claimed from the supplementary benefits scheme. The costs that may be paid include a plain coffin, transport for coffin and bearers, one car, and the fees for a simple funeral; necessary documentation, some flowers, transporting the body home within this country if he died away from home, and up to £75 of costs arising from a particular requirement of the deceased's religion. A supplementary benefits officer at the social security office should be asked for advice and help over claiming.

Presuming death

If the relatives of someone who has disappeared want to apply for a court order to presume that he has died, they must produce evidence that he is likely to be dead—for example, that he was known to have been in an area where there was an earthquake—or that they have gone to great lengths to try to find him. Usually, relatives have to wait seven years before they apply, but not if the missing person was in an aeroplane that crashed or a ship that went down. The petition is made to the high court of justice. If granted, an order giving leave to presume death is made by the court and a copy can be used in place of death certificates or as evidence before another marriage.

Disposal
The certificate of registration of death which the registrar has given to the informant must be given to the person in charge of the place of interment or cremation. No part of the certificate is returned to the registrar.

Burial
In Scotland, as in England, it is possible to purchase the exclusive right of burial in a cemetery or kirkyard plot, either in perpetuity or for a limited period. Cemetery chapels are rare. Most kirkyards are administered by the social work department of the local authority. In Scotland, a grave is referred to as a lair.

At a burial, silk tasselled cords, called courtesy cords, are attached to the coffin. Specific mourners are sent a card beforehand inviting them to hold a cord while the coffin bearers take the strain of the lowering. Courtesy cords are not used for the burial of cremated remains.

A pad or mattress is often put on top of the coffin as a development of the old custom of putting grass or straw over the coffin to muffle the sound of the earth falling on the lid when the grave is filled in.

Cremation
The regulations and procedure for cremation are the same as in England and Wales since the Cremation Regulations 1965 brought these into line with those of Scotland.

Sending a body abroad

As in England, cremated remains can be taken anywhere without any restrictions and no formal notice has to be given or permission sought when ashes are being taken out of the country. There are no formalities connected with the removal of bodies out of Scotland for either cremation or burial in another country, but you should ensure that the death has been registered in Scotland before moving the body out of Scotland. The procurator fiscal does not have to be informed.

If the body is being taken to England or Wales for burial, the certificate of registration (form 14) or the standard death certificate must be produced to the registrar there.

Bringing a body from abroad

There is no need to produce evidence for the registrar in Scotland that the death took place elsewhere. If the body is coming from England, the person in charge of the place of interment or cremation will require the coroner's acknowledgment of the notice of removal.

When a body is brought into Scotland to be cremated there, the authority of the Secretary of State for Scotland must be obtained before cremation can be carried out. This means applying to the Scottish Home and Health Department, St Andrew's House, Edinburgh EH1 3DE, with any supporting papers such as a foreign death certificate. Ashes brought into Scotland must be accompanied by a certificate of cremation issued by the crematorium.

None of the deceased's property should be sold nor, strictly speaking, given away until probate has been granted, or letters of administration. In the course of getting probate (if the person who died left a will) or letters of administration (if he died intestate), the deceased's personal representative must inform the bank, who will stop payment of all cheques and banker's orders; notify the post office, who will temporarily freeze any savings held there; and notify the tax inspector. After the grant of probate or letters of administration, the personal representative settles the debts, obtains payment of any life insurance policy, and transfers the ownership of any house, shares or other property the deceased may have had. (A detailed account of how to administer an estate is given in the Consumer Publication *Wills and probate*.)

The death grant should be claimed, and any other national insurance benefits that may be due.

The deceased's medical card should have been taken or sent to the registrar of births and deaths at the time of registering the death.

All pension books and allowance books of the deceased must be returned either to the issuing office quoted in the book or to the Department of Health and Social Security (keep a note of the pension or allowance number). If there are any uncashed orders which are due, they must not be cashed after the death, even if they have already been signed. Any unpaid amounts should be claimed when the book is returned. To get any unpaid portions of a war pension, write to the Department of Health and Social Security, War Pensions Issue Office, Norcross, Blackpool FY5 3TA, and claim the amount due, quoting the pension number. Unless the executors or next of kin make a specific claim, no repayments are offered by the Department for any outstanding pensions or allowances.

If the deceased had been an officer in one of the armed forces and a pension or allowance was being paid on the basis of his war service, the next payment that comes will have to be returned, uncashed, to the issuing office. Send with it a note of the place and date of death, and claim any amount that has become due in the period from the last payment to the death.

If income tax was being deducted from the dead person's salary under the pay-as-you-earn scheme, a refund of tax may be due, depending on the date of death and whether tax had been paid up to then. Apply to the inspector of taxes for the area where the deceased's tax affairs were dealt with; if no one contacts him about a refund, he will not do anything about it. (The executors will hear from the collector of taxes if there is any tax due.)

Since April 1980, a widow gets a bereavement allowance in the form of the married man's full tax allowance set against her income for the tax year in which her husband died and for the following tax year.

Responsibility may need to be transferred into the name of another person for a house or flat. Relatives who were living with the deceased in rented accommodation should seek advice about their rights, from their citizens advice bureau or a solicitor. (The landlord is not likely to be the best person to advise, because he may be motivated by his own interests.) Depending on her income and circumstances, a widow (like anyone else) may be eligible for housing benefit paid through the local authority to cover the rates (and the basic rent, if a tenant) for someone at supplementary benefit level. Explanatory booklets (50p each) for home owners, council and private tenants are available from SHAC (189a Old Brompton Road, London W5 0AR) and application forms are at local council offices (housing or finance department).

If relatives have to arrange to clear a flat or house quickly, furniture which is not required can be offered to a local dealer or auctioneer, and anything which is not saleable will sometimes be accepted by local charities. If you have to arrange with the local authority refuse department for a special collection, a charge may be made.

Sometimes following the announcement of a death in the papers, secondhand clothes dealers call round at the house and offer to buy the dead person's clothes. This is a simple way of getting rid of the clothes if you want to, although you will probably not be offered much for them. Remember to look through pockets and handbags before letting the clothes go. If you want to give the clothes to a charity, you will almost certainly have to pay the cost of getting them there. Some auctioneers have occasional sales of clothing. You have to get the clothes to the auction rooms and the auctioneer will send you the money paid for the clothes, minus his commission, a little while after the auction. Alternatively, you can advertise the clothes for sale, singly or as a complete wardrobe. In a similar way, other unwanted possessions of a dead person, such as books, cameras, sports equipment, can be sold by being advertised or offered to a local dealer or secondhand shop, or can be given to a charity.

When going through the dead person's belongings, you will probably find various tickets and documents. A rail season ticket should be taken to the station where it was issued and a refund claimed. If the ticket has not been used recently, either because the deceased had been ill for a long time before his death or because the ticket was not discovered until some time afterwards, the station will require evidence, such as a death certificate or doctor's certificate, before backdating the refund. A London Transport season ticket may be surrendered at any underground station or may be posted (recorded delivery advisable) to the commercial office of London Transport, 55 Broadway, London SW1H 0BD. The refund will be made from the last day of use if a medical or death certificate is produced, otherwise from the date of surrender. The refund is made payable to the widow or widower without formality; alternatively, to the executor on production of either a letter from a solicitor authorising payment to that person or a copy of the letters of administration nominating that person as executor.

Send a passport back with a letter of explanation to the Passport Office, Clive House, 70 Petty France, London SW1H 9HD, or to the passport office in Liverpool, Newport (Gwent), Peterborough, Glasgow, Belfast. You can ask to have it back, if you wish, after cancellation.

If the deceased owned a car, the registration document must be sent to the Driving and Vehicle Licensing Centre (Swansea SA99 1AR) when the new ownership of the car has been settled so that the change can be recorded. The insurance for the car, however, should be altered straightaway.

For all other insurance policies in the deceased's name, the insurance companies should be notified, and asked to cancel the policies and to refund any unexpired premiums, or to amend the policy to another name. To claim on a life assurance policy, send the policy to the company together with the standard death certificate.

There may be a refund to claim on unexpired memberships, so clubs and associations to which the dead person belonged should be told of his death and any unwanted subscriptions cancelled. Library tickets and any library books or records should be taken back to avoid getting a series of reminders and possibly a fine.

If the dead person had been getting meals-on-wheels or a home help, tell the local authority social services department that this service is no longer required, and return any aid or appliance that was on loan.

If the telephone was in the dead person's name, the executor or next of kin should write to the area telephone manager to tell him of the death and ask for the telephone account up to the date of death so that it can be paid out of the estate. Where necessary, the executor should also write to the local electricity board and gas region to cancel the deceased's contract and to ask for the meter to be read so that the debt can be met from the estate. The relevant authority should be told who will now be responsible for the account.

A number of employers run pension schemes, sometimes linked to life insurance policies. When an employee dies, some schemes provide either a cash sum or a pension, sometimes both. Find out from the dead person's last employer whether any such payments are now due.

A widow (or anyone else) who is not in full-time work and whose average weekly income is below a specified minimum can claim a supplementary allowance or pension. An explanatory leaflet (SB1) is available at all post offices and includes a claim form. An officer of the Department of Health and Social Security can be asked to call to discuss the position if the claimant does not want to go to the office to give the required information about his or her financial circumstances.

Various societies, professional bodies, trade unions and ex-service organisations run benevolent schemes for the dependants of their members or of people who qualify within the scope of the organisation. A widow should get in touch with the secretary of any organisation related to her husband's activities to find out what benevolent schemes might be available.

Cruse, a national organisation with local branches, helps widows, widowers and their children with advice over bereavement and in practical matters; details from Cruse House, 126 Sheen Road, Richmond, Surrey TW9 1UR, telephone 01-940 4818.

There is also the National Association of Widows (headquarters: Stafford District Voluntary Service Centre, Chell Road, Stafford ST16 2QA) with branches in various parts of the country. Its *Handbook for widows* (£1·50 plus postage) gives advice on stages of grief and recovery as well as on practical matters. The NAW Widows' Advisory Service includes a series of free information booklets on finance and the home.

Information about other voluntary organisations whose activities include helping people who are alone can be obtained from the National Council for Voluntary Organisations (26 Bedford Square, London WC1B 3HU) or from a local council for voluntary service. Social workers are employed by voluntary bodies such as the Family Welfare Association (headquarters: 501 Kingsland Road, London E8 4AU) and by local authority social services departments.

Each local authority is responsible for the provision of a variety of welfare services, through its director of social services. In some instances, a charge is made for the service provided, depending on the income and commitments of the recipient.

Death brings with it many problems for the family, and a social worker may be able to help at this time by arranging for practical services that are required—for example, concerning the care of children—and by trying to help the bereaved work through their often painful and complex feelings following the death.

National insurance benefits are paid to the dependants of those who paid national insurance contributions, or who had them credited while claiming sickness, invalidity, injury or unemployment benefit.

The Department of Health and Social Security administers all national insurance benefits. It issues explanatory leaflets for different categories of people and situations—for example, on widow's benefit and on the death grant—and these are available free at any social security office.

You are not expected to know what contributions have been paid or credited when you apply for any benefits. The DHSS keeps records of contributions.

The number of contributions required varies according to the type of benefit claimed. When the number of contributions does not fully qualify for certain benefits, a reduced rate may be paid. You can appeal through the local social security office if you do not agree with the decision about your claim.

Death grant
The death grant is a small sum (maximum £30). The grant is normally paid to the executors if the deceased person left a will or to the administrators if letters of administration have been taken out; otherwise, it is paid to the person meeting the funeral expenses or to the next of kin.

Following the death of a man, a claim for the death grant can be based on either his own national insurance contribution record or that of his wife, whether she is still alive or not. If the contributions of one are not sufficient, the other's may be. Similarly, for a woman the claim can be based on her own contribution record or that of her husband, whether he is still alive or not. For a divorced woman who had not remarried, her former husband's contribution record may be used.

For someone who because of mental or physical incapacity has never been able to work and pay national insurance contributions, a death grant may be paid on the contribution record of a near relative with whom the deceased person was residing or would have resided but for being in hospital or an institution.

When a child dies, a claim can be based on the contribution record of either mother or father, even if separated or divorced, or dead. Or the claim can be based on the contribution record of a person within whose family the child would have been considered for child benefit purposes. Anyone under school-leaving age, or under 19 while a full-time student or an apprentice or unable to work because of illness, counts as a child in this context.

To qualify for the death grant, the contributor concerned must have paid or been credited with at least 25 contributions before 5 April 1975 or before reaching pension age or dying, whichever is the earlier. Or the contributor must have actually paid contributions on earnings of at least 25 times the lower earnings limit in any one income tax year ending before the relevant year. The relevant year is usually the income tax year in which death occurred, but if immediately before the date of death the person on whose contributions the grant is claimed was himself dead or over 65 (over 60 if a woman), it is either the year in which he reached that age or the year in which he died, whichever is earlier. The lower earnings limit (which changes each year) is the statutory level of weekly earnings below which an employee is not liable to pay national insurance contributions.

The amount of the grant is determined by the age of the person who died. No death grant is paid after a stillbirth. For a child up to three the grant is £9, for a child between three and five years it is £15, and for anyone between the ages of six and seventeen it is £22·50. From the age of eighteen, the death grant is £30 for a man who was born on or after 5 July 1893 and for a woman who was born on or after 5 July 1898. A man who was born between 5 July 1883 and 4 July 1893, or a woman who was born between 5 July 1888 and 4 July 1898, qualifies for a reduced grant of £15. Anyone older than that does not qualify for a death grant.

The death grant has to be claimed on a form (BD1) which you can get from a social security office or applied for on the back of the certificate of registration of death (form BD8, given by the registrar for national insurance purposes). You must give particulars of the deceased on the application form and declare in what capacity you claim the grant. If you have not already sent in the certificate of registration of death (form BD8), evidence of death must accompany your completed application for a death grant. With the application form should also go the deceased's marriage certificate, if married; also any national insurance contribution card and any Department of Health and Social Security payment books not yet handed back. An undertaker's estimate or account may be required as evidence of the funeral expenses. Do not delay the claim even if all the documents are not available: the grant may not be paid unless claimed within six months of the death. If a body has been given for medical research but the relatives are going to arrange the eventual funeral themselves, the death grant should be claimed now, not at the time of the funeral.

The grant will normally be paid within about ten days, usually by girocheque cashable at a post office.

Changes to the death grant are at present under consideration by the government.

If there is no funeral (for instance, after an accident when the body could not be recovered), the death grant is none the less paid to the executors or administrators or the next of kin.

There are reciprocal arrangements between this country and some overseas ones for payment of the death grant if a british citizen dies abroad. If you need to find out about claiming a death grant or a widow's benefit after someone has died abroad, write to the overseas branch of the Department of Health and Social Security, Newcastle upon Tyne NE9 1YX.

Widow's benefit
Widow's benefit is an omnibus term used by the Department of Health and Social Security for a number of payments to which a woman may become entitled following her husband's death. A widow qualifies only if her husband's national insurance contribution record satisfies the appropriate conditions; her own contributions do not count.

Only the lawful widow can claim any widow's benefit on a man's death. If the marriage had been annulled or dissolved by divorce, the woman is not regarded as his lawful widow. She will not be paid any benefit while cohabiting with a man as his wife. If she marries again while under the age of 60, she loses her widow's benefit from her previous marriage.

A widow does not apply specifically for any one benefit but makes her claim on a detailed form (form BW1), available at any social security office or by applying for it on form BD8. On form BW1 she is asked to give particulars of herself and her husband and of any children under nineteen. She should send off the form as soon as possible and not later than three months after her husband's death in order not to lose any of the benefits. If she can send her marriage and birth certificates, too, it will speed things up.

A widow who qualifies for benefit normally gets a book of weekly orders, cashable at a post office. Each order is valid for three months and if it is not cashed within that time, you have to apply for a replacement; if not cashed within 12 months, the benefit for that week is generally lost. A widow eligible for a pension or a widowed mother's allowance can choose to be paid four-weekly or quarterly in arrear instead. She has to fill in a separate application form (in leaflet NI 105) for payment direct into a bank or girobank account or a national savings bank or building society investment account.

Widow's benefit is not affected by any earnings a widow may have or income from investments. It is, however, subject to income tax and may be affected by other social security benefits payable to her or similar payments out of public funds, such as war widow's pension or a training allowance.

If her husband's contributions were insufficient for her to receive the full, or any, widow's benefit, she will be informed in writing. She has a right of appeal to the local tribunal if she disagrees with the decision. This is explained in the notification, and a citizens advice bureau can be asked about the procedure.

National insurance benefits are reviewed by the government at least once a year. The current (November 1983) amounts for the benefits described in the following pages are on page 119.

widow's allowance
A widow under the age of sixty or whose husband was under 65 or had chosen to continue working after the age of 65 without drawing his pension, receives an allowance every week for the first 26 weeks after her husband's death, provided his contribution record entitles her to it. Increases for dependent children may also be payable.

For his widow to qualify for this allowance, the husband must have paid 25 contributions of any class before 6 April 1975 or have paid contributions on earnings in any one tax year since 6 April 1975 of at least 25 times the weekly lower earnings limit for that year. If neither of these conditions is met, the widow will not get the allowance.

An earnings-related supplement used to be payable

with the widow's allowance if the husband had paid class 1 (employed person's) contributions. Since 30 June 1982, the payment of earnings-related supplement has been discontinued.

Leaflet NI 235 explains about earnings-related supplement ending in 1982.

widow's basic pension
After the first 26 weeks' allowance, a widow without children may receive a weekly pension, depending on her age and on her husband's contribution record.

—contribution requirements
The requirements for a widow's pension are that the husband had paid 50 contributions of any class at any time before 6 April 1975 or had paid contributions on earnings of at least 50 times the weekly lower earnings limit for the payment of contributions in any one tax year from 6 April 1975. For benefit to be paid at the standard rate, the husband must have paid or been credited with contributions equivalent to the level of contributions paid on earnings of at least the minimum specified level (currently, 50 times the weekly lower earnings limit) in a specified number of tax years during his working life. For tax years from 1978/79 onwards, the qualifying level will be 52 times the lower earnings limit.

The husband's working life is normally taken to be the number of complete tax years in the period from 6 April before his sixteenth birthday to 5 April before his death, or before he reached the age of 65 if earlier. If he was already contributing to the insurance scheme before 5 July 1948, however, the period will count from the tax year in which he entered insurance or 6 April 1936, whichever is later. If he was over sixteen on 5 July 1948 and entered insurance on or after that date, the period for the calculation of his working life will begin on 6 April 1948.

The number of years required for a standard rate of basic pension are calculated as follows:

	number of years required
2 to 10 years in working life	the number of years of the working life, minus 1
11 to 20 years in working life	the number of years of the working life, minus 2
21 to 30 years in working life	the number of years of the working life, minus 3
31 to 40 years in working life	the number of years of the working life, minus 4
over 40 years in working life	the number of years of the working life, minus 5

If the number of years in which the specified minimum level of contribution is reached (known as the qualifying years) is less than the requisite number, a proportionately reduced rate of basic pension will be payable provided the condition about the minimum of 50 (or 52) payments is satisfied and that at least a quarter of the requisite number of qualifying years has been achieved.

—additional pension
The pension may include an additional (earnings-related) pension based on her husband's earnings as an employed

person from April 1978. The pension will be 1¼ per cent of his earnings between a lower and upper weekly limit (£17·50 and £120 respectively for 1978/79; £19·50 and £135 for 1979/80; £23 and £165 for 1980/81; £27 and £200 for 1981/82; £29·50 and £220 for 1982/83; £32·50 and £235 for 1983/84). If he was a member of a contracted-out occupational pension scheme, part of his widow's additional pension will be payable by that scheme.

widow under sixty without dependent children
The pension a widow gets depends on her age at the time of her husband's death.

A widow under the age of 40 at that time does not get a widow's pension.

A woman who was 40 or over but under 50 when her husband died gets a widow's pension calculated on a sliding scale according to her age. This scale starts at 30 per cent of the standard rate for a woman aged 40 at that time and goes in 7 per cent steps, so that a widow aged 49 when her husband died gets 93 per cent of the standard rate.

A widow who is 50 or over but under 60 at the time of her husband's death gets the full standard rate of basic pension.

widow over sixty
If a woman is sixty or over at the time of her husband's death and they had both been drawing the retirement pension, she can ask on form BD8 for her retirement pension to be changed to the rate for a widow. She may also be entitled to extra basic pension if her husband had deferred his retirement after he was 65. In addition, she

will receive half his graduated pension. The graduated pension addition is 3·86p a week for every unit—£7·50 for a man, £9 for a woman—of contributions paid between 1961 when the scheme began and 1975 when it ceased.

If a widow is already drawing a retirement pension based on her own contributions but a pension based on her late husband's contributions would be at a higher rate than her own, her pension can be replaced by one based on his.

A woman who is not yet drawing retirement pension when her husband dies may qualify for a widow's pension, even if she goes on working. Once she has retired, or reaches the age of 65, she inherits half her husband's graduated pension increases to add to her retirement pension as well as any of her own.

If her husband had not yet been getting a retirement pension, she receives the widow's allowance for the first 26 weeks after his death.

Under the pension scheme since April 1978, a widow can inherit the whole of her husband's basic and additional pension. If she is entitled to a retirement pension based on her own contributions, she can add the two retirement pensions together. The sum of the basic pensions is limited to the full rate of basic pension, and the additional pensions to the maximum that a single contributor could have earned from April 1978.

A man whose wife dies when they are both over retirement age can draw a pension derived partly from her own contribution record and partly from his own, in exactly the same way as a widow can do, up to the same maximum.

war widow's pension
If her husband was, or had ever been, in the armed forces and his death could be attributed to his military service, the widow should write to the Department of Health and Social Security, Norcross, Blackpool FY5 3TA, explaining the circumstances fully, and asking if she is entitled to a war widow's pension.

widow with dependent children
A widow gets an additional allowance from the date of her husband's death for each child under school-leaving age, or who is under nineteen and a full-time student or apprentice or has his schooling or apprenticeship interrupted because of illness. A widow can only claim the extra allowance for a child who was or would have been treated as part of her late husband's family, and normally only for a child living with her. This payment is in addition to the child benefit she draws.

A widow with dependent children receives a widowed mother's personal allowance for herself as well as the payment for each child. A widow who is expecting a child by her late husband gets the personal allowance and, after the child is born, the additional amount for the child.

A widow continues to get her personal allowance if any child over sixteen but under nineteen who has left school and is not an apprentice is still living with her; she does not get an allowance for the child. A widow who is under forty at the time when her children cease to qualify her for a widowed mother's allowance then gets nothing. A widow who by that time is over 40 and under 60 gets the appropriate widow's pension for her age then.

A divorced woman may on the death of her former husband get the allowance for any child in her family whom he had been maintaining. She can apply for this allowance on form CS1, available from any social security office.

—family income supplement

A widow who is in paid employment for at least 24 hours a week and has at least one child living with her under the age of sixteen, or over sixteen and still at school, may be eligible for family income supplement, if her normal gross weekly income is below a certain level. The level of income below which she qualifies depends on the number of children. Certain items of income, including child benefit but not widow's benefit, are disregarded from the calculation of the family's weekly income.

The amount of supplement payable is half the difference between the weekly income and the appropriate level, subject to a maximum. A leaflet and claim form (FIS 1) can be obtained from social security offices and post offices.

Industrial death benefit

If someone dies as the result of an accident at work or of one of the 50-odd prescribed industrial diseases, his dependants can claim industrial death benefit. Most people working for an employer and certain office-holders are covered for industrial death benefit. There are no contribution conditions for the benefit and it does not matter how long the dead person had been employed in that occupation.

In the midst of the widow's claim form BW1, there is a question asking whether she claims that her husband's death was due to an industrial accident or a prescribed industrial disease. If the answer is yes, she should send the full death certificate issued by the registrar because this states the medical cause (or causes) of death.

During the first 26 weeks of widowhood, industrial death benefit for a widow is at the same rate as national insurance widow's allowance. Thereafter, even a widow without children gets a weekly pension; if she was over 50 at the time of her husband's death, she gets a pension at a higher rate. A widow who was pregnant when her husband died or who is permanently unable to support herself also gets the higher rate pension.

A widow with dependent children of her late husband's family gets the higher rate pension regardless of her age, plus an allowance for each of the children; she continues to get this rate if she is over 40 years old when her allowances for the children cease.

A widower who is permanently incapable of supporting himself and who was wholly or mainly maintained by his wife receives a weekly pension if she dies as the result of an industrial accident or prescribed industrial disease. This is the only circumstance when a man receives a national insurance pension on the death of his wife. He should claim on form BI 200, available from social security offices, sending the appropriate death certificate and his marriage certificate.

Other dependants, such as parents or other close relatives who had been supported by a man or woman whose death resulted from an industrial accident or prescribed industrial disease, can also claim on form BI 200 for a benefit which will be either a weekly payment or a lump sum. The fact that one person is getting an industrial death benefit in respect of an industrial death does not necessarily preclude another dependant getting one, too.

Orphans

A person who takes into his family an orphaned child may be entitled to a guardian's allowance. Although the payment is called a guardian's allowance, it is not necessary to assume legal guardianship to qualify. Usually the allowance is paid only when both parents are dead, but it can sometimes be paid after the death of one parent—for instance, where the other is missing or cannot be traced, or where the parents were divorced and the other is neither maintaining the child nor subject to any liability for custody or maintenance. The allowance is not awarded unless one of the child's parents was a british subject or had been resident in this country for a specified length of time. It is paid only if the guardian qualifies for child benefit for the child.

Application for a guardian's allowance should be made on form BG 1, which can be obtained from any social security office. A claim should be submitted not later than three months after the child joins the family, otherwise the guardian may lose some benefit.

When there is no one to take charge of a child, the local authority social services department should be told and will assume responsibility for the child. If at all possible, children of the same family are kept together.

Widows and national insurance contributions
A woman who immediately before her husband died had full liability for national insurance contributions (that is, she was required to pay standard rate class 1 contributions when employed and class 2 contributions when self-employed) continues to do so as a widow.

However, if she was paying reduced-rate class 1 contributions when employed or no contributions when self-employed immediately prior to the date her husband died, she can change to full liability (but should seek advice from her local social security office about the effect of doing so). Otherwise, she continues to have reduced liability until the end of the tax year (5 April) in which her husband died if he died before 1 October or until the end of the following tax year if he died on or after 1 October.

If at the end of this period a widow is entitled to any widow's benefit at a rate not less than the standard rate of the basic national insurance widow's pension, she continues generally to have reduced liability until the end of the tax year in which she chooses to have full liability or in which her widow's benefit ceases (other than on marriage). Her reduced liability will also come to an end if there is a break of two consecutive tax years during which she has no liability for contributions as an employed person and was not self-employed.

There is no liability for any national insurance contributions after a woman reaches the age of 60.

Leaflet NI 51 gives full details of the contribution position of widows and how payment of full or reduced contributions may affect entitlement to national insurance benefits. A copy of the leaflet is issued to newly widowed women; any woman in doubt about her position can ask the staff at her local social security office for further information and advice.

A widow who has responsibilities at home, such as bringing up a child under 16, can have her rights to a basic pension on her own contributions protected without the need to pay voluntary contributions. She cannot qualify for this protection, however, for any tax year during which she has retained the right to pay reduced-rate contributions. Leaflet NP 27, *Looking after someone at home*, gives further details.

NATIONAL INSURANCE BENEFITS: AMOUNTS

The current (November 1983) weekly amounts payable for the benefits described in the preceding pages are:

widow's allowance for first 26 weeks	£47·65
widow's basic pension	£34·05
widowed mother's personal allowance	£34·05
widow's or guardian's or divorced mother's allowance per child	£7·60
industrial death pension:	
widow over 50	£34·60
widow under 50	£10·22
widower	£34·60

family income supplement:
    threshold income (1 child) per week £85·50
    higher by £9·50 for each extra child

    maximum supplement £22 (1 child)
    increased by £2 for each extra child

APPLICATION FORMS FOR GRANTS, ALLOWANCES AND
PENSIONS

BD8	from registrar, on back of certificate of registration/ notification of death	to apply for form BD1 and for form BW1, or for an adjustment in retirement pension for a widow
BD1	from a Department of Health and Social Security office, or by sending form BD8	to apply for a death grant
BW1	from a Department of Health and Social Security office, or by sending form BD8	to claim widow's benefits
NI105	from a Department of Health and Social Security office	to apply for payment of benefit direct into banks or building societies
BI200	from a Department of Health and Social Security office	for widower and other dependants to apply for industrial death benefits
CS1	from a Department of Health and Social Security office	for a divorced woman to claim allowance for child(ren) on death of former husband
BG1	from a Department of Health and Social Security office	to apply for guardian's allowance for the support of an orphan
CF9A	from a Department of Health and Social Security office	to declare choice for contribution liability
FIS1	from a Department of Health and Social Security office and post offices	to apply for family income supplement
SB1	from post offices	to apply for supplementary pension or allowance

LEAFLETS ISSUED BY THE DHSS

about payments and qualifications:

NI 49	Death grant
NP 35	Your benefit as a widow for the first 26 weeks
NP 36	Your benefit as a widow after the first 26 weeks
NI 10	Industrial death benefits for widows and other dependants
NI 93	Child's special allowance
NI 14	Guardian's allowance
NI 196	Social security benefit rates and earnings rules
NI 105	Payment direct into banks or building societies: retirement pensions and widows' benefits
NP 32	Your retirement pension
NP 32A	Your retirement pension if you are widowed or divorced
FB 2	Which benefit?
FB 3	Help for one-parent families
CH 11	One-parent benefit for people bringing up children alone
MPL 152	War widows: war pensions, allowances and welfare services

about paying national insurance contributions:

NI 51	Widows: guidance about NI contributions and benefits
NI 208	National insurance contribution and SSP rates
NI 40	National insurance contributions for employees
NI 41	National insurance guide for the self-employed
NI 42	National insurance voluntary contributions
NI 27A	National insurance contributions: people with small earnings from self-employment

NP 28	More than one job? your class 1 NI contributions
NP 27	Looking after someone at home: how to protect your pension
D 49	What to do after a death

These leaflets are available free from any social security office.

INLAND REVENUE
Leaflet IR 45 about what happens when someone dies (income tax and capital gains tax) and leaflet IR 23 about income tax and widows are available free from tax offices.

Wills and probate
is a book about wills and how to make them, and about the administration of an estate undertaken by executors without the help of a solicitor. A special section deals with intestacy and explains the difficulties which can arise when there is no will.

Wills and probate follows Matthew Seaton step by step through the tasks of an executor concerned with a straight-forward will. Reading the will, the valuation of the estate, payment of tax, the steps involved in obtaining probate, the distribution of the estate in accordance with the will, are all covered. Matthew also carries out the transfer of property to the new owner. *Wills and probate* explains clearly the procedures involved at every stage. The book also shows how to make a will—prepare it, sign it and have it witnessed.

The legal side of buying a house
explains the procedure for buying an owner-occupied house with a registered title in England or Wales, going step by step through a typical house purchase. It also deals with the legal side of selling a house.

Living with stress
helps the reader to cope with the various stresses in his or her life, brought about by job or unemployment, in marriage or divorce, loneliness, illness, bereavement. It lists common warning signs and indicates what can be done to adapt to what cannot be changed.

Living through middle age
for both men and women, this book looks at the physical and psychological aspects of being middle aged, advising on changes that can be avoided, such as putting on weight, and on minimising the effect of others. The menopause, depression, common diseases and sexual problems are discussed.

Where to live after retirement
gives advice about planning realistically for future housing needs and assessing the suitability of the present home—whether it can be adapted and the financial aspects involved. It includes detailed information on the various types of accommodation that may be available should you decide to move, weighing up the pros and cons of the alternatives and describing the criteria and methods of applying for different types of accommodation, including residential homes.

Avoiding back trouble
tells you about the spine and what can go wrong with it, concentrating mainly on the lower back. It advises on ways of avoiding back trouble and, for those who suffer from backache already, offers guidance on how to avoid becoming a chronic sufferer. It deals with causes of back trouble, specialist examination and treatment, and gives hints on general care of the back when sitting, standing, lifting, carrying, doing housework, gardening, driving.

Getting a new job
is a practical guide to the steps to take from when one job ends to the day the next one begins. The circumstances relating to unfair dismissal are explained and the remedies available. The book defines redundancy and lists your rights, it explains how redundancy payment is calculated and what can be done when an employer does not pay up. The book deals with job hunting, how to apply, what to do to get an interview and make sure that the interview goes well. It covers the points to consider when being offered a job and what is involved as an employee—the legal rights and obligations on both sides.

On getting divorced
explains the grounds for divorce in England or Wales and describes the procedure for an undefended divorce without a court hearing. It goes on to deal in detail with the practical

arrangements that have to be made, about the home, the children, finances, and how problems are settled by the court. Tax, national insurance and help from the state welfare services and voluntary organisations are also covered.

Earning money at home

is for the person who wants to stay at home while carrying on an occupation which makes some money. It explains what this entails in the way of organising domestic life, family and children, keeping accounts, taking out insurance, coping with tax, costing, dealing with customers, getting supplies. It suggests many activities that could be undertaken, with or without previous experience, and ends with advice about closing down or, more encouragingly, expanding to form a company and employ others.

Starting your own business

highlights the respective advantages and disadvantages of being a sole trader, a partnership or a limited company; alternatives such as co-operatives and franchising are also discussed. One section is devoted to exporting and makes this intricate subject easy for anyone to follow. The book deals with finding premises, finance, business income tax, and when and how to use an accountant. Throughout the book, sources of help and advice are indicated: from the government, from the local authority, from private and public organisations.

Approaching retirement

helps you approach this new stage in life with some forward planning. The main financial considerations are dealt with in detail: what your pension will be, how to invest a lump sum, how to increase your income. The relative advantages of staying in your present home and moving are discussed, and how to plan for fitness, health and making the most of your new-found leisure.

Which? way to buy, sell and move house
takes you through all the stages of moving to another home: house hunting, viewing, estimating costs, having a survey, making an offer, getting a mortgage, completing, selling the present home. Practical arrangements for the move and any necessary repairs to the new home are dealt with, and advice is given on packing and moving possessions, with a removal firm or on your own, and on the day of the move.

other **Consumer Publications** include:

Raising the money to buy your home
Securing your home
Dealing with household emergencies
Making the most of your freezer
Avoiding heart trouble
Pregnancy month by month
The newborn baby
Which? way to slim
Central heating

Consumer Publications are available from Consumers' Association, Castlemead, Gascoyne Way, Hertford SG14 1LH and from booksellers.